WOMEN TALK
MEN WALK

Dr. Wyveta Kirk

This book is not intended to replace psychological or medical advice from a licensed professional. Readers are advised to consult with a therapist regarding treatment for relationship problems. The author takes no responsibility for any possible consequences from any treatment, action, or application to any person reading or following the information in this book.

Wyveta Kirk/ SuccesSteps Publishing
www.wyvetakirk.com

Book Layout © 2014 BookDesignTemplates.com
Scriptures taken from the Holy Bible, New International Version ®, NIV®. Copyright © 1973, 1978, 1984, 2011 by Biblica, Inc.™ Used by permission of Zondervan.

All rights reserved worldwide www.zondervan.com The "NIV" and "New International Version" are trademarks registered in the United States Patent and Trademark Office by Biblica, Inc.™

Women Talk Men Walk/ Dr. Wyveta Kirk. -- 1st edition.

ISBN 978-0-9915998-0-6

ebook ISBN -978-0-9915998-1-3

Cover designed by Danielle Maait, Sydney Australia
dkmaait@gmail.com

WOMEN TALK MEN WALK

HAVE THE MARRIAGE YOU CRAVE:
GOD TELLS HOW,
HORMONES EXPLAIN WHY

Dr. Wyveta Kirk

She is a member of northside Church of christ

Dedicated to the Favorite Women in My Life.

My precious daughter, Jennifer;

Special daughter-in-law, Susie;

Cherished granddaughters,

Katelyn, Ananda, Fabiana.

With special appreciation to my patient
husband, Rod, who tolerates my long hours on
the computer and serves as my greatest
supporter.

He teaches me daily how a man loves.

CONTENTS

OUR BRAINS DIFFER

Our plane experienced a three-hour delay. My husband, Rod, and I decided to buy magazines to distract us from the long wait. At the news stand, I scanned books with covers advertising home decorating ideas and dessert recipes. After making my selection, I turned to find Rod. Unable to see him, I called, "Rod. Rod. ROD." I saw him about the time I raised my voice. He stood across the room scanning magazines on politics and sports.

What was I thinking? I knew he had no interest in books displayed in my area. He reads something in a woman's magazine only when I interrupt with, "Wow. Read this," and even then, the excerpt must be brief. I should not expect to find him nearby any more than I would wander to his section.

Men and women do not find the same things interesting. Rarely, do they think alike, and research explains why. Studies analyzing the brains of women and men show that our different amount of hormones and brain variations produce dramatic differences in what we like, our attitudes, and why we respond so differently to the same situations.

However, regardless of whose research you study, you find the sexes prove equivalent in overall performance and intelligent behavior. Disparities do not imply any functional advantage or disadvantage..

Although differences do not prove as noticeable when comparing individuals, they become significant when comparing groups of men to groups of women. You may know someone who differs from the findings, but exceptions do not invalidate generalizations. More men fit the male-type brain pattern, and more women reveal a typical female-type brain. I was told such differences fit 85% of the time.

In my counseling experience I find couples often marry someone with a brain type opposite their own. For example, if the wife appears to enjoy competitive and analytical brain activities, like ballgames and accounting, then her husband often prefers more typical female involvements, like baking and decorating. If she happens to behave as a conflict avoider, he pushes to resolve issues and enforces rules.

In fact, during my writing I became aware of an opposite pattern in my own parents. Mother enjoyed telling stories of playing basketball with the boys at recess throughout her school years, and she participated in league games long after my birth. During her Saturday basketball games, Daddy and I shared popcorn at movies. Mother worried about managing money; Daddy over-spent for special causes. After my sister's birth, Daddy fed her the 2:00 a.m. bottle. Mother took charge of landscaping. One area they shared was preparing meals. Mother baked desserts, Daddy cooked meat, and both prepared vegetables. Often, we find ourselves attracted to someone who extends our brain patterns and strengths.

However, my husband and I fit the separate male and female groupings. I have no doubt if Rod enjoyed cooking he might select a recipe book, and if I was an engineer like him, perhaps I would buy a few of his favorite magazines. But, with us, that is not the case. We fit the normal distribution range of typical gender brain patterns.

Rarely will Rod ask me to read a section in one of his books, but he frequently quotes from them. He likes action thriller movies; I prefer relationship stories. He owns five pairs of shoes and won't buy another until he discards one. I probably have 50 pair and can't pass a shoe display without glaring. He uses the GPS when driving, but he refuses to use the automatic parking feature that I appreciate. Rod buys my Christmas gift the week of Christmas, but I complete my shopping by Thanksgiving. I prefer flying when we travel so we have longer where we are going, and Rod likes driving in order to see the scenery along the way. I tend to tackle three projects at the same time. Rod focuses on one task and becomes annoyed if I interrupt with a question about a different topic. We have our own tasks we consider our responsibility. For example, Rod changes the car oil like the owner's manual recommends while I prepare our meals. Only, he loves junk food, while I push healthy meals. Our differences abound, and now scientists prove that our brain structure and hormones are the reason.

Brain and hormonal differences influence how we treat our children, depending on whether we are a father or a mother and if the child is a boy or a girl. Whether we admit it or not, boys and girls receive different treatment because they behave differently. Now research proves such behaviors are caused by brain and hormone functioning. In addition, how we relate as a couple deeply impacts our children. Children analyze us continually, and all decisions we make impact them.

Although understanding the opposite sex is baffling at times, we are not so different that we can't learn to appreciate our dissimilarities. The brain and hormone studies offer new ways of thinking about relationships and understanding why we act as we do. The new information can help us better appreciate the opposite sex.

Research, when applied, helps a wife avoid frustrations when her husband fails to respond as she wants. It explains why her husband responds like most men would in the same situation. It confirms that his behavior carries no intention of hurt or distrust. He just responds differently than a woman. Of course, the reverse also holds true.

I am a woman who has made multiple relationship mistakes. My desire to learn better ways of relating challenged me to continue my education and become a psychologist. Before in-depth study and hours of counseling couples, I did not understand what makes a man tick. I learned a lot from counseling couples, and I write for women who might benefit from current research, and the generic comments couples shared during therapy. They explain why a man rarely acts like a woman wants. The following chapters describe my counseling experiences of working with multiple couples combined into two stories. I never counseled a person named Kaylie, Dan, Judy or John but chose these names to ensure confidentiality of couples I did counsel. I hope the information helps you avoid some pitfalls I tumbled into, and hope you remember to turn to the Lord during the times you do stumble.

I find the brain and hormone studies complement God's instructions of how He wants us interacting. In fact, the more I study, and the older I grow, I realize how scientific research validates God's commandments and find that scientific research offers an understanding of why God asks that we treat others in loving ways. Therefore, this book addresses the ways brain and hormones cause us to relate. It touches lightly on how our marital relationships impact our children. And it shows how research findings help explain why our Holy God provides the instructions for us that He does.

Rod and I believe in God, Jesus Christ, and the Holy Spirit; however, we differ in how we strive to serve others because of our love for the Lord. We both acknowledge that God's commandments are written for our good and how striving to live by the Lord's commands ensures relationship success.

TECHNICAL TERMS

Acetylcholine (Ach) is a neurotransmitter in the central nervous system (brain & spinal cord) involved in arousal and attention and in the peripheral nervous system that helps activate muscles.

Adrenal Glands are located one on each kidney. The outer part of the gland releases cortisol and aldosterone and the inner releases adrenaline and noradrenaline.

Amygdala is an almond shaped mass located deep in the temporal lobe of the brain, involved in the processing of emotions. Responsible for what memories are stored and where they are stored, determined by how intense an emotional response is invoked.

Axon is a threadlike part of a nerve where impulses move from a cell body to another cell.

Cognition is the mental process of acquiring knowledge and understanding through both our senses and thoughts.

Cognitive thinking is the conscious intellectual process of attending to something and deciding how to act in response.

Cortisol is significant in understanding this book. Cortisol is a hormone that is secreted into the blood stream by the two adrenal glands and is regulated by the pituitary gland. Cortisol supplies rapid burst of energy for confronting fight-flight situations when we feel stressed. Under normal conditions, our cortisol level lowers during sleep, increases when we wake to arouse us, and varies to meet the demands of our day. Our level of cortisol impacts our serotonin and dopamine levels. When cortisol is high, they remain low and vice versa. A prolonged increase of cortisol contributes to depression, disrupted cognitive functioning, food cravings, fatigue, and sleep loss.

Dopamine is both a hormone and neurotransmitter that is involved in cognition, motivation, sleep, attention, voluntary movements, memory, and mood.

Fight-Flight describes behaviors we use for self-protection. With fight, we yell, call our opponent rude names, and insist we are right. With flight, we withdraw emotionally and often physically and refuse to speak for hours or days.

fMRI These machines map which parts of the brain are involved when performing mental tasks by detecting changes in the way the brain consumes oxygen to meet blood flow demands. It illustrates how the brain processes words we hear, images we see, odors we smell, and sends messages from one area of the brain to another.

Gray Brain Matter consist of numerous cell bodies and capillaries in the brain where information is processed and stored. Men have more gray matter and think more using gray matter.

Hypothalamus is part of the brain responsible for the production of hormones that control sleep, hunger, temperature, and sex drive. It signals the pituitary gland when specific hormones are needed by the body.

Neuron Sensory neurons take signals from outside the body and carry them to the spinal cord and brain. Motor neurons take signals from the spinal cord and brain and turn them into gland and muscle actions.

Neurotransmitter carries signals between neurons and other cells.

Oxytocin (ox-ee-toe-sin) is another significant hormone discussed in this book. It is often referred to as the calm-connection or love hormone. It lowers our cortisol levels, thus reducing the stress symptoms associated with fight-flight attacks. It is also involved in child birth and breast feeding. The hypothalamus produces oxytocin and stores it in the pituitary gland. Men and woman have approximately equal amounts. This hormone calms us enough to think how to best protect ourselves during times of danger. Our level of oxytocin increases when we are with someone we like and make eye contact, share intimate talks, and touch physically, especially sexually.

Personal Correspondence indicates I emailed the author, whose work is discussed, telling the person what I wanted to say regarding their research. Some responded with a simple approval; others suggested comments which I used.

Pet Scan imaging uses radioactive traces of a special dye that measures the blood flow in body organs.

Pituitary Gland is the master gland. It influences how other glands operate. It is located in the center of the skull and manufactures eight types of hormones.

Testosterone is a hormone made in the testes that's responsible for maturation of the male sex organs, facial hair, sex drive/function, muscle strength and bone strength.

Serotonin is a neurotransmitter that influences mood, hunger, sleep, and arousal. An undersupply is associated with depression.

Temporal Lobe is one of the brains four lobes located on the lower side of the cerebral cortex and is associated with long-term memory and emotional responses. It contains the hypothalamus.

Thalamus is located above the brain stem and relays information from our senses to the cerebral cortex.

Vasopressin is a hormone responsible for controlling our volume of blood.

White Brain Matter is tissue in the brain containing nerve fibers, most of which are insulated axons. It has few cell bodies. Women have more white matter and use it for making communication connections.

CHAPTER ONE

UNCONDITIONAL LOVE

Tears ran down Kaylie's cheeks. She sat quietly for several seconds. I handed her a tissue, but she ignored it. Tears dripped on her skirt as she began. "I kept losing weight. I wasn't trying. I don't eat much when my husband, Dan, travels, but I never lost like this before. Then the cramps started. They even woke me at night. Finally, I went to the doctor, and he ran numerous tests. I was surprised - no shocked - when he told me the results. I couldn't believe it. I have terminal ovarian cancer, and cancer has spread to other areas. He says I have three months. Maybe less. I had no idea that a Pap smear didn't test for this. Just a few months ago, my Pap test was normal."

"I had no one to tell. I couldn't tell Dan on the phone and our girls are too young. I have no other family." Kaylie paused and sat quietly for several minutes. "I do my best to hold myself together and take the girls to school without them seeing me cry. Afterwards, I cry and pray all day."

"Then Dan's return home hit me with a second blow. Before I could tell him I have cancer, he insisted he needed to tell me something. He admitted that he's involved with another woman and wants a divorce. I almost fell out. I couldn't breathe for a few seconds. I just fell backwards into a chair and stared at him. I couldn't even speak. Then I asked him to give me two days to adjust to such shock and phoned you for emergency counseling. Honestly, I never saw this coming."

Kaylie sought my assistance to win back her husband. She did not want to die with them estranged. She wanted better memories for her daughters than their parent's separation. I asked if she was prepared to act loving, even at the expense of pride and self-respect. Kaylie stated that, at this point, she had nothing left to lose. Desperate, Kaylie agreed to every suggestion I made.

Kaylie promised to focus on each day and not let worry about tomorrow ruin the time left with her family. She committed not to let Dan's behavior determine how she reacted and pledged to respond with love no matter what Dan said or did. Kaylie agreed to make no promises to Dan but show him how she was changing. If she made a promise and slipped, her error could become Dan's excuse to bolt. We discussed why she should not act clingy, plead, or make any demands. When a spouse desires to leave, the partner's clinging or begging often makes the spouse run faster and use the partner's apparent weakness as justification. Demands, for example, can make a man react stubbornly to prove he cannot be controlled. Nor was Kaylie to yield to Dan's efforts at manipulation or react if he threatened to take the children and leave her penniless.

Counseling couples, I find affairs tend to burn out within weeks. Some take months, but with time, the intense emotions of the affair subside as the illicit partner's flaws surface. If the spouse will act loving during this time, the spouse appears more and more desirable as the preferred marriage partner. If they agree to remain together and work through their marital problems, they tend to look back at this time and realize how the openness that was required to resolve their issues made their relationship stronger.

I explained to Kaylie that affairs are rarely about sex. More often the straying partner's emotional hunger to feel desired, special, or needed is ignored at home and met by the illicit partner.

Kaylie and Dan had what I call a cool relationship. They rarely argued. They tended to hide frustrations and hurts, and talked primarily about their children's activities. They seldom touched, except for infrequent, routine sex. From Kaylie's comments it became obvious that Dan felt lonely and unappreciated as a man. Kaylie needed to satisfy Dan's void of emotional and physical contact and have him feeling emotionally full.

However, time was not on Kaylie's side. She did not have months to wait for the attraction of the other woman to subside. She needed to maximize every remaining minute. Keeping Dan at home and away from the other woman proved essential while she learned to satisfy Dan's needs. She needed to forget the other woman. Asking questions about when, what, where would only increase her hurt. The more she knew the deeper her pain. She needed to ensure she supplied Dan's needs and kept herself strong, rather than centering her thoughts on the other woman. She didn't have time to work through additional hurt which could only come with more details. With such little time remaining, Kaylie needed to use whatever words would keep Dan at home. Positive togetherness would prove Kaylie's best offense.

Kaylie asked Dan to continue living at home for six weeks and watch a movie with her each evening. She planned for them to view humorous movies and then shift to emotional love stories. This was recommended because research shows that a person's stress reduces and their hopefulness increases by watching humorous films. Humor inhibits negative thoughts (Vilaythong, Arnau, Rosen, and Mascaro 2003). Kaylie needed better control of her anxiety and a sense of hopefulness so she could follow the remaining suggestions.

As their movies moved to more serious stories, Kaylie was to increase the ways she touched Dan, and to flood him with praise. She promised that no critical words would pass through her lips. Regardless, of what Dan said or did, she would return a kind comment. Kaylie needed to convince Dan that he could find the same fulfilling love at home. Loving unconditionally proves challenging but possible.

When I asked Kaylie how Dan might react to her condition, her answer surprised me. "I don't plan on telling him. I don't want him staying out of sympathy. For sure, I don't want him staying with me while wishing I would hurry and die so he can be with the other woman. No, I am not going to tell him. I have no other family. My parents are dead, and I am an only child. At least for now, you are the only one who is to know."

To solicit Dan's agreement to remain at home, Kaylie promised, "I will not challenge the divorce if you agree to do two things. First, do not leave us for one month. Give me that much time to calm, adjust to the idea, and prepare the children. Second, come home at your usual time, eat dinner as a family, then sit with me on the sofa each evening and watch a movie. After I spend my days thinking about divorce, I need the distraction of a movie at night so I am not acting negatively while the girls are home. Help me keep things normal for them while I try to adjust. After one month, I will agree to anything you ask. I won't make an ugly scene for the girls to remember. We will work through this peacefully. I will even try to help the girls like the other woman. I know it will be better for them if they do." Reluctantly, Dan agreed.

When Dan told the other woman of the arrangement, she protested and insisted they should be together. Dan explained that he promised Kaylie to avoid negative incidents in front of the children. He wanted to ensure the kids accepted her. He reminded her that, in one month, they could be together permanently.

Kaylie appreciated that months earlier she switched her work assignments so she worked from home because after seeing Dan and their daughters off each morning, she needed to return to bed for a while. Two weeks later she resigned without telling Dan. Tasks that previously seemed easy, now consumed tremendous energy. Meanwhile, she showed her daughters how to sort clothes for doing laundry, how to prepare their favorite casserole, and how to write thank you notes and address envelopes. Kaylie helped the girls memorize her favorite Scriptures, the ones making her days bearable. She hoped the passages would comfort her daughters after she passed. There were so many things she wanted to teach them.

Kaylie made a list of movies that she asked Dan to rent. The first week they watched comedy. One evening while laughing, Kaylie hugged Dan and whispered in his ear, "It seems that somewhere along the way we forgot how to laugh together, doesn't it?" When Dan removed his shoes, Kaylie grabbed his feet and gently massaged them. After a couple of evenings, Kaylie began pressing her body against Dan's as she sat closer. The fifth day, she asked Dan if she could lean her head against his shoulder and explained how tired she felt. Dan shrugged but did not protest.

Dan noticed Kaylie's weight loss. He knew when she became upset that she tended to eat less, and he attributed it to his asking for a divorce. He concluded her red eyes meant she cried a lot. Dan assumed correctly. While alone, Kaylie cried often. She cried because she would miss all the events she wanted to share with her daughters, their graduations, marriages, children.

When thoughts crept in about Dan being with the other woman, Kaylie immediately prayed and asked God to replace them with thoughts of Dan's positive qualities, and God responded. She then asked God to forgive her for wanting to dwell on thoughts that could only cause more damage to her family.

Kaylie remained determined to have her last days with her family be ones they remembered as pleasant, not ones filled with grief. While home together, she refused to dwell on the future. She basked in every minute left and enjoyed their togetherness. She refused to allow her limited timeline or negative emotions to control her thoughts. She thanked Dan for everything he did to help her, regardless of how insignificant it seemed.

Within days, when Dan turned on a movie, Kaylie leaned against him. Occasionally, she took his hand and rubbed his fingers and arms. If they watched a sad movie, she buried her face in his shoulder and pretended not to cry as she stroked his neck.

Week three, Kaylie asked Dan if he would hold her while they fell asleep, something he had not done in years, maybe not since having the girls. While Dan held her, Kaylie prayed aloud for Dan and their daughters to know how much she loved them.

Dan felt annoyed hearing Kaylie's prayers. He thought she wanted to manipulate him, but he said nothing. How could he object to Kaylie closing her prayers with, "Lord, let Dan and the girls forgive the times I mistreated them or ignored their needs. Instead, have them think only about how much I love them." While alone, she prayed, asking God to help Dan forgive her of the ways she failed as a wife and mother and for him to marry a woman who would love their daughters.

Dan had no idea that Kaylie faced limited time. She wore blouses hanging outside her skirts in an attempt to hide her continued weight loss.

During the fifth week of Kaylie's requested period for Dan's staying home, he began to look forward to their movie time. Even their daughters giggled and teased, "We have to go to bed so you two can cuddle and love, don't we?"

The following weekend, Dan made a drastic decision. He decided to end his relationship with the other woman. He left work early and stopped by the woman's condo. When she opened the door, she flung herself at Dan, wanting to be held. Dan pushed her upright and told her he was not going to divorce his wife. He resolved to make his marriage work. The woman reacted vehemently, "You are one low life, Dan. You are nothing but a loser, and a liar. Stay with that cold witch you married. You deserve her." She was still screaming when he walked out the door.

Dan rushed home. He wanted to tell Kaylie. She said nothing when he announced his decision. She just wept softly and hugged him.

That night they watched another movie. Only tonight they kissed and made love. Afterwards, Kaylie's prayer carried a deep plea for the girls and Dan to remember always how much she loved them. Kaylie related that this proved her happiest week ever.

Two weeks later, Dan woke to find Kaylie asleep in bed. Dan seemed surprised because she tended to be in the kitchen with coffee prepared when he woke. Only Kaylie was not asleep. Kaylie died during the night.

On Kaylie's nightstand, stood an envelope addressed to Dan. She placed the letter on the stand every night and then hid it when she awoke, so Dan and the girls did not see it. She replaced it after they left for the day. Her note explained her terminal condition and why she refused to let Dan leave and create bad memories for their daughters. Her death would prove upsetting enough, and Kaylie wanted their last memories filled with love. She insisted that Dan should remarry. He needed a wife and the girls needed a mother. Her note assured Dan that her prayer for his new wife, whoever she would be, to love the girls as much as he did was genuine. Kaylie wanted Dan to know that she died happy and thankful for having married him.

Emotions Do Not Need to Control

Dan deserved punishment, and Kaylie wanted to react angrily. She considered tossing Dan out of the house. She thought of multiple mean names to call him. Bitter words and rudeness raced through her thoughts when she spoke, but she bit her tongue. She refused to speak her thoughts. Certainly, she felt like treating Dan as he deserved, but she vented in my office, not at home. Gradually, her anger dissolved as she and Dan increased their closeness

A woman experiences a strong desire to retaliate when she feels betrayed, but Kaylie refused to let her emotions control her behavior. She knew if she responded to Dan's sinful behavior with sinful words their relationship would disintegrate totally. Kaylie did not want to become a mean person. She refused to allow fight or flight responses to control her thoughts or influence her character. Her goal remained to love, and praying ensured that love controlled her thinking.

Kaylie refused to allow anger to cloud her judgment. Instead, she admitted how she contributed to Dan's straying. She had given more time to the girls than to him. She put their needs ahead of his and placed the girls and her career before Dan's emotional needs. The spark present in their early days died years ago. Her estrangement with Dan created his fertile desire for an affair. Dan needed emotional and sexual intimacy, and she remained unavailable. With only a month to live, Kaylie did not have time for denials or excuses. Facing death demands truth.

Kaylie reacted with blunt honesty. Dying is not a time for worrying about pride or self-esteem. Kaylie wanted to make things right with the Lord and with Dan, and that required a self-evaluation, with repentance of flaws and sins.

Kaylie knew if she reacted with hostile behavior, Dan would likely leave immediately. Another woman who treated him with respect and kindness waited eagerly for his return. No man stays when hammered with harsh, bitter anger, even if he earned such treatment.

Instead of reacting negatively like she felt, Kaylie repeatedly thanked Dan for staying with her and the girls and honoring her request. She expressed appreciation for all he did around the house and showered him with praise for being a thoughtful father and provider. When she hugged him, she clung tighly for minutes. She treasured every remaining moment of their togetherness. Kaylie filled Dan's emotional needs that the other woman previously provided. Kaylie said and did what is spiritually and intellectually the right way to behave. Showing maturity, Kaylie made an intellectual-mental decision to act lovingly and to respect Dan as he needed.

However, what changed Dan's decision was not just that Kaylie became a sweet, kind woman as she was before they had children. Her cuddling and touching Dan in loving ways triggered good feelings in him. The hormone, oxytocin, helped him feel good as they flooded his brain.

A man experiences strong hormonal induced feelings when touched in loving ways. As Kaylie shifted from sitting close, to laying her head on Dan's shoulder, to lightly kissing him, and cuddling in bed, he felt better and better. Oxytocin flooded his brain, and he credited Kaylie for his positive feelings. At long last, she satisfied Dan's emotional needs with respectful words and warm, physical touches.

Had Kaylie not included gentle progressive touching, it is likely that Dan would have still left. He would have experienced tremendous guilt as he should for straying, but still, he would have felt drawn to the other woman. The other woman made him feel good about himself and she couldn't keep her hands off him.

However, once Kaylie filled Dan's intimacy needs, he did not want to leave. Kaylie was his wife and the mother of his children. This was his home and where Dan wanted to stay.

With the Lord's help, Kaylie proved that a dead relationship can be revived by one spouse. It remains easier when spouses work together, but one spouse can often mend a broken marriage.

If you desire a relationship like Kaylie and Dan shared during their last days, you can make it happen. You can do it with or without your spouse's help. It will take longer than it did with Kaylie because she faced, not one, but two traumatic emotional situations. Such distress either forces immediate change or you go with the flow and allow others to control your fate. Kaylie made the choice to salvage her marriage, and you can make your marriage great too.

Few of us encounter such trauma as Kaylie. For us, change and adjustment take time. Unless faced with a traumatic episode, change rarely happens as a one-time event or quick occurrence.

Kaylie proved that regardless of how negative our feelings, we can manage how we respond. Emotions do not need to control how we behave, nor do another's actions. We are capable of feeling one way and acting another. We can give unconditional love, no matter how we feel.

You can choose to create the marriage you want. You, too, can have the marriage of your dreams. You can choose to have one like Kaylie ultimately experienced, or you can follow the crowd and accept one like your many friends who live estranged. If you choose the former, you will learn how by reading the intimate details of John's and Judy's marriage in the following chapters. They required hours of counseling but eventually, they turned a stormy relationship into a marriage that both cherished. Their personal details explain how they overcame multiple, but too often typical, relationship obstacles. Their lives show how to create a marriage that too few people experience, but could. The choice remains yours.

CHAPTER TWO

WHEN STRESS OVERWHELMS

John grabbed the telephone receiver on the first ring. Frank his supervisor sounded urgent, "Can you come to my office? Right now?"

Before John closed Frank's door, Frank blurted, "We have to let you go, John. The business isn't making money like it was, and we have to let several of our employees go. We can't keep doing business as usual, or the business won't survive."

John slid slowly into a chair. His thoughts raced violently. He wanted to insist that his current project needed his skills. Instead, he froze. He could not speak. He sat staring at Frank in disbelief. His heart pounded so loudly he could hear it above Frank's words. John did not attempt to say anything; there was nothing left for either to say.

John's eyes filled with tears as he staggered back to his desk. He felt woozy. His sweaty hands trembled. How could he tell his wife? What about the project on his desk that was weeks from completion? He closed his office door and leaned back against it. "Why does my mouth taste like burnt coffee? Why am I thinking of such a stupid, unimportant thing like that right now?" Then John realized he was speaking aloud with no one to hear. Suddenly, he feared he might be sick. He decided to go home. Obviously, his work here no longer needed him. Besides, he could no longer think about work.

John replayed Frank's words all the way home. John knew the company struggled, but he did not realize layoffs would be extensive enough to include him. Although Frank assured him that his termination had nothing to do with his skills or talent, such comments did not help. Flattery would not pay a mortgage or buy groceries. John could think of nothing but their many bills.

Likewise, Judy, John's wife, was surprised and fearful. She, too, thought only about how bad things could become. "We shouldn't have bought the new car, John. At least our savings would last longer if we didn't have a car payment." Judy squeezed her eyes shut and tried not to cry.

"I figure we have enough savings to last four months. Five or six if we watch every penny. I will find another job by then. Meanwhile, I can draw unemployment. It isn't what we are used to having, but it will help. If things get really bad, we will sell the car. We can get by with one automobile with me not working." John tried to reassure Judy but his words sounded more like he hoped to convince himself.

Judy possessed few job skills. She worked at low-paying jobs when she and John first married and stayed home once they had children. John supported the family financially. Early in their marriage, they agreed this was the lifestyle they wanted.

While they did have a small savings, Judy feared the money might not last long enough for John to secure other employment. She could think of nothing but how dire their future might become and how she possessed limited work experience to help. If she mentioned her concern, John cut her off with, "I'll take care of things. You don't have to worry." Such words left Judy feeling isolated, not comforted.

John withdrew into his own private thoughts, rarely talking to Judy or the children. He spent his days on the computer and telephoning friends about job openings. John's busy routine increased Judy's anxiety. John coped by withdrawing and ignored how inaccessible he became. His flight from the family left Judy feeling abandoned.

Distraught, Judy needed to get out of the house for a while and be near people. She attempted to soothe her emotions by going shopping. She purchased several items for their children and charged a large amount. At the mall, she felt better, but afterwards, her negative feelings returned. She wanted someone to blame, someplace to direct her anger.

Eventually, John received the larger than normal credit card bill with Judy's recent purchases, and his stress level spiked higher than he could handle. Inflamed, John used a fight approach to regain some control as he yelled at Judy. "How could you spend so much money? Maybe I should stay home with the kids and let you make us a living. Maybe then you would know how to manage money. For sure, you wouldn't buy things the kids don't need. You know we can't continue living as we did. What's wrong with you?"

After attacking Judy, John raced out the door, shifting from a fight attack to a flight maneuver. He could hear Judy screaming as he slammed the car door.

"You're the loser, not me! It's not my fault you lost your job. The kids still need things. Why did I marry a man who doesn't care what his kids need?" Crying, Judy stomped from the room.

Judy counter-attacked John with hurtful words, instead of explaining the reasons for her purchases. Then she chose a flight response and raced from the room. She flung herself across the bed and flooded her mind with thoughts of how John did not love her. "If he loved me, he would appreciate my trying to keep things as normal as possible for the children."

Parental Fights Impact Children

When parents address each other with fight and flight defenses, they negatively impact their children. Children recognize parental anger, and they learn how to handle strong emotions by observing mom and dad. When parents protect themselves by hurling insults at each other, racing away, or refusing to speak, they ignore what their behavior models. They disregard children's need to feel secure while their home reeks with hostility. When angry, partners think only about themselves and their pain, not what their children learn or feel.

Fight and Flight Create Worse Feelings

John's and Judy's flight and fight responses increased their estrangement. Such behavioral choices were chosen as a way to push the offender away as they hoped to protect self. Both sought distance from their source of hurt and used cruel words and physical distance to increase and protect their private space.

When faced with genuine physical threat, flight and fight prove appropriate. However, choosing such responses while disappointed, frustrated, hurt, or angry create a deeper disconnect from the ones we love. Withdrawing or attacking the other never resolves an issue. Instead, both feel worse.

When we choose a flight-fight defense for self-protection, our partner tends to immediately retaliate. If we attack our spouse, he wants to hurt back as if someway it lessens his pain. If he chooses a fight approach, he retaliates by escalating his voice and assaults with hurtful, exaggerated words, as we did. If he chooses a flight tactic, he withholds love by leaving or punishing us with the use of silence for hours or days.

We ignore that we intentionally inflict pain on our partner, and rarely do we calmly explain why we feel hurt and ask if our interpretation is what the other meant. Sadly, we choose revenge and increase our own anguish. Regardless of whether we employ fight or flight, such counterattacks never make either feel better.

Worse, when we choose a fight-flight reaction, we operate in sinful ways because the episode shifts from being a test to a temptation. We tend to fail by choosing to respond from the anger within our hearts, instead of love. Such trials could allow God to mold us more like Jesus' image, but too often, we choose wrongly.

Scientific research helps explain such behavior. When a man feels stressed, his brain receives an increase of blood in his right cortex and a reduction of blood in his left cortex (Wang et al 2007). When a woman becomes overly anxious, her limbic system produces less of the hormone serotonin, and she feels worse. She self-protects, and her negative mood outlasts the stressful episode (Walderhaug et al 2007).

The hormone serotonin that helps us feel happy also contributes to reason and calmness. But when our serotonin level lowers we no longer control our aggressive behavior and our mood darkens.

When we feel angry and fearful another is going to hurt us, the sympathetic system, a branch of the autonomic nervous system, signals the adrenal glands to release norepinephrine, epinephrine, and cortisol. These hormones attempt to cope with our increased stress level. They reduce our sensitivity to pain and provide quick bursts of energy. We prepare for fight or flight. Too often we think only about self-protection. While we think acting this way will protect us, it never does. If instead, we chose to face the current test with a desire to understand why our spouse acted as he did, we avoid a battle, respond lovingly, and both feel better.

We must remember that not only does our spouse observe our bad behavior, God watches too. He not only hears our words, He knows the secrets in our hearts that drive such conduct (Psalm 44:21).

Overly-stressed, We Seek Support

John chose a flight response to his unexpected termination at work. He chose to go home for two reasons. He wanted to leave the environment where his stress hormone, cortisol, was increasing and causing his mood and thoughts to worsen. However, more than avoiding the situation at work, John wanted comfort from Judy. Feeling rejected at work, John sought Judy's acceptance. Dr. Sian Beilock (2010) explains that spouses who act supportive serve as stress vaccines for each other. Being comforted by the spouse reduces the stress created during the emotionally charged event. However, if the spouse fails to show sympathy, the stress level increases and can turn dangerous. An extended elevated cortisol level causes some brain cells to dysfunction which creates multiple health issues (Fillit 2010).

When a charged situation becomes uncontrollable, like John's termination, a cortisol hormone imbalance takes the longest time to recover. Thus, John left work desperately needing Judy's support.

Giving Others What's Wanted for Self

Clearly, John's job loss contributed to the current problems in his and Judy's relationship. However, the loss of income affected them differently, and their resulting reactions are explainable.

Instead of giving what Judy needed, John offered her the support he wanted for himself. He withdrew and became quiet. He focused on finding employment and tuned out all distractions so he could create a plan. Louann Brizendine, author of *The Male Brain* (2011), explains that when a man faces a personal problem, he applies his analytical brain structure to find a solution while women use emotional thoughts (personal correspondence 8/27/12). Analytical reasoning and emotional thinking produce very different behaviors.

Likewise, Judy focused on her own desires. She pressed John to involve her more because she believed it would reduce her anxiety. She longed to explore possible locations where John might pursue jobs and to discuss the impact each place could have on the family. His being too busy to talk left Judy feeling rejected. She reacted to rejection feelings with strong emotions. She thought only about what helped her feel better and never considered how she could provide the support John needed.

Thus, Judy and John failed each other. The focus on self left both feeling isolated and lonely amid the crisis. They cared, but they failed to deliver support in ways that sustained the other. Both focused on self, the wrong target.

When Shopping Helps Women Feel Better

Judy immediately worried about the impact their financial loss would have on their children. Focusing on her children ensured their home life remained fairly normal, and it kept her from dwelling on her fears. Judy felt abandoned by John while he searched for a job. They rarely spoke. She missed people and felt isolated.

Judy's shopping trip temporarily improved her negative mood because being around others in a pleasant environment increased her hormone levels of oxytocin, serotonin, and dopamine. Filled with these, she felt better. Her shopping trip served as a reprieve from stress at home. She briefly forgot money worries and how seldom John interacted with her or their children.

Research explains that when a person feels anxious and sensitive to rejection, they experience a drop in the hormone progesterone and compensate by seeking other social contacts (Maner et al 2013). Judy satisfied her desire to be with others by going to a mall because people are always present. She used the children's need for school clothes as her excuse. However, if offered the opportunity to participate in John's activities, Judy's progesterone would increase, and she would no longer experience a strong desire to be with strangers.

A majority of women describe experiencing a cheerful, positive mood while shopping. They consider it a pleasurable experience. However, they often feel guilty later about their spending (Pine and Gnessen 2009).

Shopping for most women proves a joyful experience because she absorbs the entire experience. She glides up escalators, lingers beside fragrant smelling perfumes and samples some along the way, and gently rakes her fingers across fabrics while she meanders through the clothing department. A woman makes a purchase only after examining every item to ensure she buys the nicest at the best price. She enjoys looking at new and different items and observing other shoppers. She may even chat briefly about an item with a stranger. Her lingering shopping experience increases the production of her good-feeling hormones, oxytocin, serotonin, and dopamine.

John could not comprehend why Judy would go shopping while he was unemployed. He failed to understand that being near others in a pleasant environment helps a woman feel better. Few men understand this because men shop uniquely different. If a man needs something, he rushes to the store, grabs what he needs, and hurries to leave (Wharton's Jay H. Baker Retail Institute). He came to buy a specific item, and when he finds it, he has completed his shopping. He has no interest in looking at other displays. Nothing in such a brief shopping experience gives a man's brain time to produce the good-feeling hormones that women receive while leisurely shopping.

Women's Needs When Stressed

Men and women attack problems differently and in ways that reduce their own tension. A woman desires active involvement and equates participation with feeling loved and exclusion as rejection. She cares how change impacts her family, especially her young children. A woman focuses on today's worries while a man concentrates on long-range goals. He pinpoints all the information needed for achieving his goal and briefly stops thinking about the problem once he makes a decision. However, she cannot stop worrying until the issue resolves.

A woman eliminates anxiety by feeling engulfed in loving support. She receives an emotional boost by talking and talking and talking, but not about the weather or sports as men tend to discuss. For a woman, emotional support consists of sharing private, personal details and how she feels about each. She craves having private information about her man. Without enough intimacy, a woman questions the quality of her marriage. However, for a man, intimacy involves touching, especially sexual touching and sharing enjoyable activities. A woman cannot comprehend desiring sex if she has not talked first, so she feels connected intimately. She bonds before sex by talking; he connects during sex when he feels desired.

Ask a woman what makes a marriage successful and she will likely say, "Communication. A couple needs to stay current." Judy believed this too. She yearned to have John put his arms around her and explain every detail of his job search. She wanted to hear his ideas, dreams, and fears. Judy wanted them to share a mutual plan, rather than John having one that left her in the dark. When she thought John withheld her desired connection, Judy became upset and believed that his silence meant he did not love or trust her. Talking about John's job search represented more than factual data for Judy. For her, it symbolized emotional connection.

Therefore to feel better, Judy needed an opportunity to express her fears, and together prepare ways they would cope if the worse situation happened. Because Judy focused on problems, collaboration proved essential, and without it, her stress lasted longer.

To ensure Judy felt loved, John needed to talk openly and frequently. However, for him to attempt to provide such verbal support would have him believing that Judy created an emotional and physical overload.

Men Reduce Stress Differently

Men do not reduce stress like women. Rather than addressing current, daily concerns, a man concentrates on longer-term matters. He prefers to work alone and assigns more importance to the information required for carrying out a decision. Once completed, he temporarily releases the worry from his thoughts by distracting himself with other activities. A man curtails his negative thoughts while a woman ruminates about problems.

Judy thought about the daily effect the loss of income made on her children; John fixated on finding adequate earnings. Therefore, if they worked together, they would have covered all considerations.

What John failed to realize is that by addressing Judy's fears, she would feel relieved and be more supportive. John's discussing solutions would have reassured Judy that she can trust him to provide for their family. If John supplied Judy emotional support, she would believe that he can succeed financially. John could help Judy feel a partner in his job search by affirming, "If I have to go through a job change, I'm glad I have you by my side." He would need to define what having her by his side meant to him because, likely, his meaning differed from hers. But she would feel appreciated.

However, John did not need multiple discussions to feel loved. Long talks only increased the drama in his life. Like many men, John's self-esteem hung on his career success and financial well-being. Losing them brought depression.

Men who are happier with their finances tend to describe happier marriages. A man feels loved when he knows his wife respects him for all the support he provides for her and their children.

John needed to hear that Judy believed in him and respected his ability to support the family. He wanted to know she believed he would find other employment and trusted him to keep them afloat. The last thing he needed was for Judy to call him a loser or question his talent. John doubted his own ability to find adequate employment when Judy spoke such words. When Judy made degrading comments, John shut down emotionally. He could not speak. Instead, he sought ways to avoid her. Judy's fight attacks raised his cortisol level, which increased his stress and deepened his depression more. John took flight to avoid feeling worse.

Therefore, to feel better John required messages affirming, "You know you will find other work, even better than the job you had. It's because of your expertise that we have savings to tide us over. We will be fine because of how well you manage money. I know it." John also needed praise, especially now, for helping around the house, even though severely stressed.

Like Judy, John experienced fears of their unknown future, but he could not share them while feeling unappreciated. He feared Judy would think he was not doing enough or not doing the right things. John's fear of Judy responding with criticism out weighted his worry of finding employment, so he kept his ideas to himself. He required Judy's respect before he could share his plans and fears. He also needed her to remind him that his termination was not personal, and the business failing was not because of anything he did. Once John believed Judy intended to be supportive and believed in him, he would no longer pretend that everything's okay. Then, Judy would serve as John's stress vaccine.

Seeking Assistance

God tests couples daily to learn to give love in ways the other needs. In John's and Judy's case, all the financial tension added to the challenge. Sadly, not all couples choose to meet their spouses' prerequisites for connecting emotionally and physically. Instead, they wallow in self-pity and direct their frustration at each other, like Judy and John behaved for several weeks.

Fortunately, Judy sought counseling, and later, John joined her. They needed to learn to handle frustration and anger without using fight - flight approaches. Regardless of how fearful their circumstances seemed, God held a special plan for them. While turmoil ruled their home life, the havoc would not destroy them once they learned to rely on the Lord and each other.

CHAPTER THREE

GOD'S DESIGN FOR FAMILIES

"**M**ommy, are you sleeping with me tonight? If you are, I need to move my big teddy bear." Judy's young daughter knew from experience that when her parents quarreled her mother often slept in her bed.

Sleeping apart modeled a bad example for their children, and it prolonged Judy's and John's estrangement. But after John yelled at her for spending so much money, Judy did not care and chose a flight defense. She thought only about wanting distance from John. Separateness let her ignore her need to apologize for spending so much money without first discussing their children's needs, and it hindered John from asking forgiveness for his angry outburst.

Their emotional detachment worsened that evening when John and their son disagreed, and Judy interrupted to defend the child. John told their son to mow the yard, and the son protested that he had too much homework. When John told the son he could do homework after mowing, Judy interrupted, "No. Go to your room and do your homework right now. Homework is more important than mowing a lawn. You dad was wrong to insist. Go in this house. Homework comes first." Still angry, Judy used her son as a weapon to continue punishing John.

John snapped back, "Okay, have it your way. Raise a son who thinks he shouldn't help with chores. I will do it instead of working on resumes."

Power of Bodily Contact

Judy could sleep alone, but she chose to sleep with her daughter because hugs and warm bodily contact with someone we like increases our level of the good-feeling hormone oxytocin. Judy's oxytocin boost improved her mood and reduced her stress. Feeling better, she ignored her guilt feelings for how she behaved.

However, Judy's sleeping arrangement fostered other problems. First, sleeping apart ensured there would be no apology and make-up sex, and men crave spontaneous sex. Men act more loving to their wives after sharing sexually, so Judy missed John's warm embrace that could have short circuited their discord and left them feeling connected again.

Second, when Judy cuddled the daughter throughout the night, the daughter became accustomed to the good feeling her increased level of oxytocin provided, and she protested when Judy eventually returned to John's bed. The children received mixed signals about how married couples love and fight. When children learn to accept fight – flight strategies as normal, they tend to mimic these patterns in their own marriages and suffer similar discord.

Third, Judy starved John of his much needed oxytocin boost. Already stressed, John's bad mood increased with Judy's rejection. He slept restlessly and woke more irritably. He acted less supportive of Judy, and became annoyed with their children's typical noisy behaviors, rather than enjoying their companionship. Research shows when a father plays with his children, they both experience an increase in oxytocin and bond more closely (Geddes 2009). Therefore, Judy's dysfunctional sleep practice interfered not only with her reconnecting with John but the closeness of John and their children.

Our brain supply of oxytocin helps explain why God expects a couple to put each other before their children. Putting the spouse before all others is a significant aspect of the marriage nuptials, and God instructs us to keep all vows.

Directive for Creation

After God created Eve, He told Adam and Eve how He wanted families structured for ensuring their success and happiness. Genesis (2:18, 24) explains God created woman to serve as man's helper, and He intended them to bond tightly. "For this reason a man will leave his father and mother and be united to his wife, and they will become one flesh." (Genesis 2:24). God provided the rule because solid, secure marriages are the central foundation of a home, a country, and the world.

However, the uniqueness of God's instruction for Adam and Eve must not be overlooked. Adam and Eve had no father or mother to leave, and it appears they had yet to share a sexual relationship and had no children to send on their way. Rather, God prepared Adam and Eve for when they became parents by telling them what makes a healthy family and good parenting. God mandated that their relationship with each other should hold greater importance and be more intimate than any other. He wants a husband and wife securely bonded and their relationship given a higher priority than the relationship with their children, even when they argue and feel estranged.

The Lord's commandments remain the same today. Scripture explains that Jesus Christ is the same yesterday, today, and forever (Hebrews 13:8). Because the Lord does not change, neither do His instructions. God expects parents to rear their children to become independent, God-fearing adults, and implementation begins shortly after the child's birth. Parents plant the seed of faith in their children's hearts so the Lord can make it bloom. However, without parents striving to live as a good example the plant rarely blossoms.

God First

Immediately after Adam and Eve birthed two sons, Scripture details the sons sacrificing to the Lord. Likewise, honoring God, regardless of any required sacrifice, remains a requirement for us. Such teaching runs from Genesis through Revelation. Jesus says if we love father, mother, son, or daughter more than Him we live unworthy of Him (Matthew 10:37). God wants to hold first place so He can mold our hearts to be like Christ's.

Our first priority remains the Lord. We respect His Lordship by frequently praying, depending on Him rather than self, studying His Word, and revering Him while alone and with others. And researchers Mochon, Norton, and Ariely (2007) confirm that such actions increase our oxytocin levels. Our reverence for the Lord shows in how we choose to live. What we choose to eat, how much we eat, how we dress, jobs we pursue, how we treat our co-workers, entertainment we engage, how we spend money, and how we set priorities all reveal how much we respect the Lord. The essence of worship strives to have our every thought, word, and action honor, love, and revere the Lord. Only when we make Jesus the Lord of our lives does He promise to be our Savior.

Spouses after God

God wants to hold first place in our lives, and second should be our spouse. We become one with our spouses and no one else. We remain bonded, regardless of what sacrifices such a union requires. Swallowing our pride and sleeping together when upset reduces our stress hormone cortisol, raises our feel-good hormone oxytocin, and reduces our emotional disconnect. Body contact throughout the night creates an intimacy that bonds us tighter.

Together we commit to rearing our children, so they know the Lord and are capable of leaving us. However, the primary role in a family should not be held by a child. Both parents care for children's needs, but the focal point of every minute of time or every dollar of money does not go to children.

When Judy took her son's side against John's telling him to mow the lawn, she weakened her relationship with John and damaged their children. The son learned he can control and divide his parents. Circumventing John's authority taught their children they have authority that is not rightly theirs, and they develop an inflated idea of their role.

Second Place Husbands

Some women think their husbands understand when they put their children first, but my counseling experience proves they hold a flawed belief. Even if the child has special needs, a husband must remain first. Otherwise, she risks him distancing himself from a child who needs him the most. A second-place husband tolerates this position only so long. Eventually, he begrudgingly leaves emotionally if not physically. He either reaches outside the marriage for someone to fill his emotional needs or invests his time and energy in some drug or a favored child.

Such a wife can be spotted by how she speaks about her husband. He might say, "Did you miss me?" and she responds, "Nope. I was too busy." Or, he might boast, "I am really happy about how it turned out," and she replies, "Only because of my involvement." While it appears a subtle or humorous message, most often, it's an honest evaluation of her feelings. She never misses an opportunity to reduce him. Yet, she boasts loudly about her children. In elusive ways, this represented Judy.

Unfortunately, when a wife remains reluctant to put her husband above her children and meet his needs, my counseling experience finds that she becomes resentful of others who do make him feel good. In his jealousy and abandonment, he turns to others to feel needed, and she becomes critical of these people. Her criticism pushes him away further. No husband continues takes the side of a wife who belittles him over someone who helps him feel valued.

Secondary Wives

Sadly, the wives who make a husband secondary to their children often become the very women who express hurt if their husbands treat them in similar ways. If the ignored husband turns to a child, especially to a daughter, for his needed attention, the wife feels a sting of pain. If he buys gifts for the daughter, but not his wife, she watches silently – but uncomfortably. If he accompanies the child to school events and the wife cannot also attend, she feels displaced and jealous. She wants them sharing the child's events together or for the child to go with peers, not be left behind without her mate. Then she experiences guilt for having thoughts about losing her spouse to her own daughter.

A wife wants to hold first place with her husband, and if she feels displaced by a husband's favored child, she gradually withdraws from this child. They never bond closely as they normally would. She pours her energy into their neglected children or her career, and the family never develops as God intended.

Ultimately, a second-place spouse of either gender feels insignificant and slighted, and their marriage remains an afterthought rather than the central foundation of a loving home. Research finds men experience more jealousy if their wife is sexually unfaithful; yet, they, too, feel jealous if they find themselves in second place to a wife's emotional attachment. However, research finds women find emotional infidelity as the more distressing event, and it matters not who the other party is (Buss, Larsen, Westen and Semmelroth 1992).

When we suffer with a bout of jealousy we experience a chemical imbalance. The amygdala and the anterior cingulated cortex (worry and caution centers) become turned way up, while the hormones that help us to love (oxytocin, dopamine, estrogen, and testosterone) are turned way down (Brizendine 2007). The hormonal changes hinder the ways we concentrate and how we think about our partner. If this effect continues long-term it produces serious side effects. Yet, the spouse rarely focuses on relieving their partner's feelings of jealous.

Emotional Neediness

Emotionally needy couples create an over-bonding with their children in an attempt to fill the hole in their hearts. Because they do not obtain enough support from each other, they turn to a child in hopes of feeling needed and valued through the child's accomplishments. Having a child they can boast about proves extremely satisfying.

These couples ignore that no human can satisfy all of another's emotional desires. Completeness is God's role, and only He supplies all a person needs. When God lives first in one's life, no huge emotional void remains. A mate needs to satisfy only a minuscule hole.

From hours of counseling couples, I find that when detached couples put their children ahead of each other, the marriage rarely lasts until the last child leaves home. But when it does and the last child leaves, both spouses feel alone, empty, and bitter. They blame each other for the loneliness in their lives. These couples suffer the empty nest syndrome to a worse extreme. Some cling to an adult child and interfere continually in the child's life. Some divorce and remarry, but the next marriage rarely survives because second marriages share additional problems with step-children.

To save their marriage, a couple must take the attention off their kids and allow Jesus to place their thoughts on the importance of their relationship. Otherwise, the children end up in a single-parent home and become the ultimate losers.

Love for a child is not allowing the child to sleep with a parent, or having one parent take the child's side against the other parent. Love to a child is security of having a stable home free of worries. If you genuinely love your children, give them what they need most: Their daddy and mommy living together in a peaceful and loving house ten, twenty, fifty years from now. If you genuinely love your children, they will remain in third place.

God asks to reign first in our lives and second our spouses. Third place is for minor children. Once grown, children drop to a lower position so they can become one with their new mates without our interference.

Anytime we think we know how to rear children better than God, we create marital conflict. Worse, when we deliberately disobey God's instructions, we sin because sin is stubbornly doing things our way rather than God's way.

How different their marriage would be if John and Judy held a goal of giving their children to the Lord all the days of their lives. Their children would never be used for satisfying their own emotional needs or as a weapon for hurting each other. They would treat each other differently if they questioned how their own behavior determined their children remaining close to the Lord.

Judy definitely needed to establish priorities and return John to his rightful place in the family. Another major challenge was for her to learn to disagree with John without their disagreements turning into attacks. Judy agreed. However, she first needed to realize what unrealistic expectations she held for marriage. That was our next task.

CHAPTER FOUR

SOUL MATE FANTASY

" Sometimes I wonder why John and I married. I dated a lot of other men and maybe I should have married one of them. None of them withdrew into a shell when things weren't going their way. John and I were madly in love, but maybe we just weren't meant for each other. I know neither of us seems happy right now."

A woman expects more from marriage than a man, and Judy proved no exception. When her expectations lagged too long, an argument brewed. She quietly absorbed frustrations until she could no longer control her feelings. Then she blamed John and blasted him with unkind remarks. Hurt, John tended to withdraw, but if backed into a corner, he returned rude, aggressive words. However, John rarely began arguments. The conflict over Judy's shopping proved a rare exception. When frustrated, John ignored it by telling himself that this, too, will pass. Sometimes, his delay worked.

Unlike women, men spend little time evaluating the condition of their marriages. A man feels satisfied knowing his wife and kids are safe and secure, but that rarely satisfies a woman. She craves intimacy and sleeping safely under a shared roof is not enough for her. She wants emotional closeness, and for her, it requires knowing what is happening in her husband's life.

If a woman's emotional cravings go unmet for an extended period, often, she fantasizes about another man who better meets her needs. She may not focus on a specific man; rather he may be an ideal imaginary person. However, no man admitted such thoughts during any of my counseling sessions. He might have an affair and become hooked emotionally on the woman, but he did not fantasize constantly about how much better his life would be with her.

Many women espouse a desire to find their own special soul mates, and, of course, they describe a man who fills their every emotional craving. Like Judy, they insist, "If only I had chosen a better man, I would not be having the problems I am today. I want one who makes me feel loved." She believed another would make her feel that way. Frustrated, Judy attempted to force John into a mold that conformed to her fantasies. She wished for a closer connection than most men could maintain. Judy described John as far removed from an ideal soul mate.

Judy's imagining a perfect soul-mate provided reasons for continually focusing on John's shortcoming. She claimed he failed to meet her expectations for being a good husband; yet, she expected John to know what she wanted and what helped her feel loved without telling him with examples. Judy needed to realize that John did not reject her desire for closeness, but rather, he had no idea what she wanted. His brain processed her words in ways that produced a different meaning about what bonding required. John had no clue what Judy meant when she told him she wanted him to act like a soul-mate. When her wishes failed to materialize, she became frustrated, and conflict erupted.

Women, especially those with low self-esteem like Judy, expect marriage to bring them total fulfillment. They marry anticipating their husbands will solve all their problems, without realizing they can't. Eventually, many divorce in hopes of finding better mates. However, when a disillusioned woman remarries, she transfers all of her disappointments to the next husband, and eventually experiences similar frustrations. Each time, she believes she marries Prince Charming and later thinks he changes into the Big Bad Wolf. She yearns to be treated like Cinderella and have a man sweep her off her feet, fill her every desire, and change her life in positive ways. She forgets that fairy tales end when the princess and prince meet. They do not detail problems of daily living when money runs short and in-laws arrive for a month's stay.

Judy entered counseling insisting that John needed to be repaired. She did not come to change her own way of relating. She claimed, "John is selfish. He agrees to talk, but before we are half finished, he gets up and walks away. Obviously, he doesn't care about my feelings or he would want to know what bothers me." Feeding her mind such messages, Judy became disillusioned with their marriage and faulted John completely.

Judy needed to realize she erred in believing, "It's all John's fault I am unhappy," and stop thinking her life would be wonderful with another. She could divorce John and remarry, but likely she would choose a second husband with qualities similar to John's because she finds his traits attractive. Her next man might not have the same annoying habits, but he would have other undesirable qualities that, perhaps, John doesn't. Regardless of whom she married, she and another husband could never experience perfectly aligned ideas. They, too, would encounter conflicts because not every difference has a resolvable solution. Even in the best of marriages, couples experience two or three issues that remain unresolved after 20 - 30 - 50 years. They learn not to let different opinions determine the quality of their relationships.

Finding a new partner sounds appealing when a woman credits all her problems to her husband's failing. However, once she accepts her own shortcomings, she realizes that both need to make adjustments.

Eventually, Judy acknowledged how she frequently met John's attempts to share details with, "Why didn't you do this?" and how such bossy responses stifled his desire to talk more. She admitted that such responses invited John's withdrawal, which contributed to her feelings of loneliness. She acknowledged that she would bring the same personality traits into any succeeding marriage because she did not know how to break this destructive habit. She accepted that, without change, she would be dooming any marital relationship.

Sadly, Judy's own lack of commitment triggered many of her complaints because when a woman lives genuinely committed, she accepts less than perfection and forgives her husband's shortcomings. When truly loyal to her man, a woman pays the price to ensure their relationship succeeds; a man does the same for a wife he commits to loving. If committed, Judy would value her marriage more than any issue where she and John disagree and keep their problems in proper perspective.

Such honesty proved difficult for her, but Judy finally admitted that she rarely gives 100% to John. She lives holding back, but she expected, even demanded, that John give fully.

Rejection Hurts

Many women say fear of rejection has them withholding love for self-protection. They believe they hurt less if not fully involved. This shows in how they refuse to be totally open and share what they think about all matters. Instead of speaking up when first frustrated, they wait until bothered by multiple issues, and explode over something unrelated to their real concern.

Regardless of her reasons, when a wife chooses flight and avoids connecting with her husband, she creates pain in him similar to serious physical problems. Functional magnetic resonance imaging (fMRI) brain scans show a rejected man experiences actual physical pain and not just emotional discomfort (Kross et al 2011).

Judy never considered that selectively withholding love caused John to feel such discomfort. At first, she wanted to argue that she could give completely to another man because they would not have a history of hurt. However, when asked how many years it might take before she and another man created a similar history, she could not answer.

Judy tried to deceive herself into believing she would give 100% to another man, but her current personality would not allow it. With her first serious frustration with a second husband, Judy would likely react using her typical fight response of angrily yelling, making demands, or calling him rude names. Otherwise, she would select a flight response and bury herself in her children's activities, dismiss their estrangement, and ignore her husband's needs. Either way, Judy would withhold the love required to make her marriage successful and be headed for a second divorce. For genuine change, Judy needed to acknowledge her own behavior that required correction and learn to appreciate why John reacts differently. With change, she and John can learn to share fully with each other.

Finding the perfect partner is not what guarantees a happy marriage. The idea of finding a perfect soul mate remains a misnomer. For a successful marriage, both parties must work to become the type person the other likes living with and surrender self-wills to God's will.

Cohabitation Isn't the Answer

Nor does a good marriage result from a couple living together before marrying to decide if they are compatible. No two humans are compatible – until they willfully alter behaviors for pleasing the other, and this takes years, not a brief stint of togetherness. A long-term relationship requires a binding commitment because no couple becomes totally compatible.

Areas of difference always exist. Without a commitment to both the partner and the relationship, one party leaves with the first strong disagreement.

In cohabitated relationships, the couple bonds on sexual attraction and good feelings, rather than a commitment to forming a long-term relationship. Because emotions fluctuate, they lose that high feeling of euphoria with the first signal of serious distress and begin looking at who else might be available. Then, the person sprints and eventually, finds themselves attracted to another. They enmesh in another sexually attractive, romantic relationship. Each party judges the relationship by how 'I feel while I am with you,' not on developing long-term togetherness. Compatibility cannot be created in a series of short relationships. Creating harmonious togetherness requires a life-long process of making frequent changes as a couple matures.

The Bible resonates with benefits of serving another, not finding someone who makes us happy. All of God's commandments explain how to have good relationships, and research helps clarify why God condemns living together without marriage (Exodus 20:14; Matthew 5:27; Mark 7:21). Research reported in the *Journal of Social and Personal Relationships* by Dush and Amato (2005) documents how married couples experience the highest sense of happiness and well-being. Marriage produces higher self-esteem, greater life satisfaction, and less stress. Married couples feel better about themselves and their relationships.

Successful marriages begin with the exit door bolted shut. People dwell on their partner's positive attributes, and these virtues keep them drawn to the person. A commitment to remain together for a lifetime creates the relationship, and no sacrifice seems too much.

Love comes from giving. You don't love your toddler because she gives to you; you love her because of all you do for her, and it helps you feel needed. So it is in marriage. The more you serve your spouse, the happier you feel.

Self-defeating Cycle

God created Eve to be Adam's helper. No other place in Scripture indicates that God created one special, ideal person for making another happy and fulfilled. If He had, wouldn't we eventually find the right person? Surely, by the time we married multiple times one of our marriages would last. However, such a belief is also fantasy. The divorce rate in America for first marriages ranks near the 50% mark. Couples in second marriages experience a failure rate close to 67%, and third marriages end in divorce 74% of the time (Forest Institute of Professional Psychology cited in Divorce Rate).

The odds of creating a solid, loving marriage and avoiding a life cycle of constant upheaval improve by paying the price to succeed with your current spouse. To beat the odds, learn to love your husband in ways he values and teach him how to love you. Tell him what you desire and explain why it matters. Frequently ask what you can do to make your marriage better for him. Your children benefit because no second or third spouse loves your children like their biological parent.

Reconnect after Arguing

After an argument like the one over her shopping trip, Judy must demonstrate a large amount of affection to have John reconnect with him so depressed. Therefore, she needed to hug John daily, tell him something she appreciates about him, and thank him each time he does something helpful. Currently, John feels horrible as a provider and needs to hear that Judy values him for more than earning money.

God wants us counting our blessings, not thinking about what is missing in our lives and hunting someone to blame. He does not want us tolerating our spouses or fantasizing about another. God wants us depending on Him for making our marriages dynamic.

Judy could list her blessings, but she remained unprepared to tell John all she appreciated about him. She required additional counseling before she changed her focus and realized his many positive traits.

CHAPTER FIVE

SADNESS IS CONTAGEOUS

"I understand John being depressed. He works long hours sending resumes to companies in hopes of finding work. What he fails to realize is how his being sad takes a toll on me too. He doesn't worry about our financial condition any more than I do, but it's the way he acts that is getting to me. I am not sleeping well. I cry a lot and dread each day because I know it will be more of the same. In three months we are going to be broke. I offered to find a job, but John threw a fit. He would rather borrow money from his parents than me work. Only he has forgotten how controlling his mother can be about money. I do not want any part of borrowing from her. While it's not what I want, I will leave John if he takes money from his mother. His mother's controlling intrusions and John's withdrawal would be more than I could handle." Judy responded to John's depression with similar behaviors. Her reaction is quite common; rarely is one spouse traumatized without it impacting the other.

In fact, trauma, fear, and extreme psychological stress negatively impact women to a greater extent that men. When exposed to traumatic problems that lie outside their typical range of experience, women suffer more severely. The most frequent and debilitating psychological disorder after a traumatic episode is post-traumatic stress disorder (PTSD), although rates for depression and anxiety remain very high too.

After a serious stressful event, women and girls experience more negative symptoms. They describe a lingering sense of fear and dread, loss of control, worry, anger, numb feeling, sleeplessness, nightmares, intrusive memories, avoidance of people who serve as reminders of the event, bouts of anger, and flashbacks of what occurred (National Center for Post-Traumatic Stress Disorder). In a multi-nation study of children as young as 14, females suffered twice as often as males after serious threats of violence, bullying, death of family and traffic accidents (Elklit and Petersen 2008). After a seriously distressing situation, women face a greater risk of depression and alcohol use (Breslau et al 1997).

Long-term Study of Terror-related Stress

A classic example of a disaster leaving people with a high rate of post-traumatic stress disorder (PTSD) is the bombing of the Alfred P. Murrah Federal Building in Oklahoma City on April 19, 1995. At the time, this was the most severe incident of terrorism in America. Almost half the people inside the building died, including many children. Approximately 90% of the others suffered an injury. Property damage ran in the millions (North et al 1999).

However, this traumatic event impacted survivors differently. Firefighters and medical professionals who responded reported few psychiatric problems, although they worked directly handling the injured and deceased (Robert Wood Johnson Foundation report, 2007). These workers credited their stamina to support from family and friends (Crocker 2005).

Women suffered significantly more psychiatric disorders than men. Forty-five percent of the women experienced post-traumatic stress, which was twice the 23% rate for men. Women experienced more symptoms of major depression,

32% vs. 13% for men, and the rate for generalized anxiety disorder was 9% for women, with no man suffering this disorder. Percentages remained the same, regardless of a woman's level of education and marital status. A psychiatric diagnosis of two simultaneous disorders proved prevalent in women, with most experiencing both PTSD and depression (North et al. 1999).

Research using fMRI scans reveals that the higher the quality of the person's marriage, the less threat-related neural activation people experience during a disaster (Coan, Schaefer, and Davidson 2006). Having family support proved a significant factor in Oklahoma. The overall divorce rate was significantly lower during this period than the previous ten-year trend (Nakonezny, Reddick, and Rodgers 2004).

The learning from the Oklahoma bombing emerged into prominence after the September 11 World Trade Center attack. Again, a significant finding revealed that a human-caused distress resulted in greater psychiatric impairment than a natural disaster, and women suffered the most severe disorders (Robert Wood Johnson Foundation report 2007).

The 9-11 World Trade Center experience left many survivors with a hyperactive amygdala as revealed by research conducted three years after the attack. The closer a person lived to the twin towers, the more activated the person's amygdala remained (Ganzel et al 2007). Six months after the 9-11 attack, women were the ones who remained fearful and continued having nightmares (Goodwin, Wilson, and Gaines 2005).

Under duress, women do prove psychologically weaker. When fearful, a woman's brain does not function like a man's. PET scans of men's brains reveal that the right amygdala lights up when they watch graphically violent films, but in women the left amygdala fires. The hypothalamus, which helps to activate a person's fight or flight response for self-protection, increases the cell connections in the brains of women but show little effect on men (Cahill 2005). Fearful, a woman's first reaction is to seek protection.

Findings from more than 40 studies of school shootings in the U.S. since 1990 reveal similar findings. However, it appears that depression, not PTSD, becomes as the primary disorder, with school girls suffering significantly worse (Johnson 2012). Research also finds college students experience a spiked increase in alcohol and drug use after shootings on college campuses. Perhaps, this is how college students hide their fears.

While severely stressed, women respond as the weaker sex emotionally and physically. Research reports women exposed to traumatic stress show significant evidence of inflammation caused by an overactive immune response that results in cardiovascular disease and arthritis, even years after the stressor. This effect remained after the researchers adjusted for depression, anxiety, and PTSD. This finding led researchers to predict that women with multiple stress exposures have increased inflammatory response more often and for longer periods than men (Neylan et al 2011). Scientists confirm that women with stress symptoms prove more likely than men to develop a stronger reaction to fearful situations (Inslicht et al 2013). The researchers suggest that women may reflect a pre-existing vulnerability or it may arise in ways specific to women.

Stress-Induced Depression Is Contagious

Following a stressful event, many men and women take months or years to improve. Many never recover. POWs of World War II and the Korean War still suffered with depression forty years after the wars ended (Engdahl, Page, and Miller 1991), and this is not unique to the United States. Only half of Israeli POWs in the 1973 Yom Kippur War never recovered from depression (Solomon, Neria, Ohry, Waysman, and Ginzburg 1994).

Certainly, losing a job, does not compare with a POW's experience. However, John's termination did prove traumatic for both he and Judy. His firing was unexpected, and the delivery of the message was handled poorly. What causes a debilitating reaction in one person, may not for another.

Wives of Traumatized Men

Research of contagious depression comes primarily from war veterans and finds women frequently encounter a secondary trauma effect when their husbands return home. The more stressed her husband, the more often a wife develops the same or similar psychiatric symptoms, and the more their marriage suffers (Dekel and Solomon 2006). Research in other countries produces similar findings. When Australian POWs returned home depressed, their wives experienced depression that correlated to their spouse's (Dent et al 1998). Israeli veterans admitted having intimacy problems in their marriages, and rarely disclosed their feelings (Solomon, Dekel, and Zerach 2008). Living with a veteran who suffered stress problems caused a wife to become enmeshed in her husband's pathology (Lyons 2001), and she experienced greater generic psychological disorders (Renshaw et al 2011).

Depression and post-traumatic stress of one spouse proves contagious for the other. The more they disclose their feelings the better their improvement and the less a spouse experiences secondary traumatization. The strongest protective factor remains spousal support.

Women demonstrate great strength in their ability to be open and vulnerable verbally. They share their deepest, darkest emotional secrets much easier than men. However, a woman becomes the weaker sex when confronted with shocking situations for which she has no normal way of coping or for remaining healthy when her husband becomes depressed and refuses to discuss his feelings.

Women Value Protection; Men Protecting

Women place high value on knowing their husbands will protect them from hurt and the fear of being harmed, and men seem programmed to act as protectors. It is another example of the Lord's complimentary creation. For example, when the USAir plane landed in the Hudson River in NYC, passengers panicked. That is, until a crew member yelled, asking that women and children be allowed to exit first. With that cry, everyone exited calmly according to "What Went Right: Flight 1549 Airbus A-320's Ditch into the Hudson" in *Popular Mechanics*, October 1, 2009 issue.

A man's hormones program him for risk-taking. As a man's fear increases, his testosterone and stress hormone, cortisol, activate his amygdala. These hormones provide the aggressive energy he needs for taking action. A man's hormones equip him for risking his own life and protecting others (Brizendine 2011). When police and firefighters raced into the Twin Towers on 9-1-1, they weren't just saving a person, they were saving America. Soldiers in war zones aren't only saving their own lives, they protect their buddies, and know they are protecting their families back home.

Jesus Didn't Choose a Woman

Jesus did not select a female as one of his chosen apostles. Clearly, a woman teaching Jesus' message would have received little respect during that culture. However, regardless of that day's societal acceptance, women did accompany Jesus and the apostles, and some women even provided their financial support (Luke 8:3). But few women would have endured beatings, threats, and jail time like the apostles encountered because anxiety is four times more common in women (O'Brien, 2008). Facing such threat and duress, a woman would likely abandon Jesus' work. With too much fear, a woman becomes emotionally handicapped. She seeks safety, not confrontation.

God forewarned husbands to expect such reactions in wives and instructed husbands to treat their wives with respect as the weaker partner. A wife wants to know she is protected, provided for, and relieved of extremely stressful situations. To treat a wife any other way hinders the husband's prayers (1 Peter 3:7) because when he fails to treat her as God requires, they tend to argue instead of praying and seeking help from the Lord.

Feeling Valued, He Acts Helpful

A wife needs to tell her husband how she values his protecting and providing for her and not wait for a crisis. Hearing her admiration makes him feel good about himself and honors the Lord's commands (1 Corinthians 10:24).

I challenged Judy to tell John each time he does something that leaves her feeling valued and protected, like when he refuses to let their children speak disrespectfully or refuses to allow his mother to intrude. Judy needed to see John's positive qualities, and he needed to hear the ways she appreciates him. When John felt potent in their marriage, he wanted to use that strength to care for her. So, in the long run, Judy benefited the most.

I assured Judy if she doubled her efforts she would cherish the payback. But, her reward is not unique. All of the Lord's commandments make our relationships successful as more and more research confirms, and as Judy would learn in future sessions

CHAPTER SIX

WHY HE BEHAVES AS HE DOES

"I can't take John's isolation any longer. I feel abandoned, and I am angry. It's like the kids and I live in the house with a ghost and this ghost never speaks. It's not our fault John lost his job, but we are being punished. He just mopes around all day with a sad face. He hasn't borrowed money from his mother, but keeps mentioning it as a possibility. It's about the only thing he does say anymore. Just implying that he might take her money makes me want to grab the kids and run." Judy shrieked.

Judy tolerated John's quiet treatment as long as she could. She knew they could not solve their detachment without discussing it, so she demanded to talk. Judy insisted that talking would help her feel included and closer to John.

However, chills ran down John's spine when he heard Judy's tone. He did not know what he had done wrong but feared another heated dispute was brewing. Judy's insisting, "We need to talk," reminded him of the many times they argued and ended up sleeping separately, with tension peaked the following morning. John believed a talk session would entail a long list of all his shortcomings. Yet, what Judy desired was for John to validate her feelings. She wanted validation more than she cared about hearing how his job search was coming because reassurance that he understood why she worried proved that he cared about her feelings.

By now, John joined Judy in counseling, and he explained, "I feel tremendous pressure. I don't need Judy making constant demands. If we argue, we go days without speaking and that adds to my stress. The kids see we aren't getting along, and I worry about them too." He hated Judy insisting they should talk.

John admitted, "Sometimes, I know when an argument is brewing. I sense when Judy's annoyed about something. I don't say anything and hope the problem will go away or she'll get over it. I see no need to bring an argument to a head if it isn't necessary."

We spent considerable time discussing if he preferred worrying about an impending explosion or if he would rather calmly confront the issue. Ultimately, he agreed to tell Judy when he knew something bothered her. He agreed that he didn't want her to remain upset, and he wanted to resolve whatever troubled her. His taking the leadership, rather than waiting for Judy to force the issue reduced his stress and worry of what lay ahead. John also discovered that by his putting his arm around Judy and asking to discuss what upset her reduced the negative way she talked. Usually, all she required was for him to validate her feelings, not discuss them for hours. It was the times he missed or ignored her distressed signals that their discussions turned into arguments.

Why Men Hate Emotional Talks

During counseling, it becomes obvious that many men dread talking on an emotional level with their wives present. Privately, when I ask why, they admit fearing if they say what they think then their estrangement will worsen. He knows from years of experience that he cannot communicate on an emotional level like she does. Women blurt out what's on their minds; men think before responding. Women speak with more emotional overtones, while men use communication more for influence. Men talk freely in public settings, but most of their discussions focus on objects, activities, and facts, not on themselves. Never on feelings.

The hormone testosterone helps a man slam on his emotional brakes. Boys receive conditioning at an early age not to show their real feelings. According to Louann Brizendine, author of *The Male Brain* (2011) boys learn not to cry or show strong emotions. As men, they feel safer not saying anything than attempting to deal with an emotional wife. He does what he thinks is best for himself and believes he's incapable of supplying what she wants.

A man competes, plays rough, and obsesses with rank and hierarchy. His life centers on who wins, but when it comes to communicating on an emotional level, many husbands know they will lose, And he's not losing to someone stronger or larger. He loses to a woman. Therefore, he seeks to avoid verbal contact. Like these men, John tended to sit withdrawn in hopes the issue would disappear.

Many men hesitate before talking to avoid feeling vulnerable. They fear they are not all they think a man should be. They want to appear macho, but fear they come across as unmanly or incompetent (Goulston and Goldberg 2002). Men experience insecurity as often as women. Therefore, a man takes the safe road, shuts down, and keeps quiet when it comes to discussing personal intimacies. He fails to realize how his withdrawal increases his wife's distress. She wants to talk – and right now. He believes that talking will erupt into a bigger argument so he avoids making things worse. Yet, the more he withdraws, the more she needs to talk. Both want what helps them feel better. If he learned to validate her feelings, their talks would short-circuit.

What's Different about Her?

Women enjoy conversing because of their biological makeup. The corpus callosum, the bundle of nerves connecting the right and left hemispheres of the brain, is larger in women. This increase in connections gives women a verbal advantage because a woman's brain organizes language on both the left and right sides. Louann Brizendine, author of *The Female Brain* (2007; personal correspondence 8/17/12), explains that when a woman discusses emotional topics, more areas of her brain activate than a man's. She finds pleasure in talking because of how she was created. A woman thrives on repeating stories, giving advice, having secrets, and asking questions just so she can share her own ideas on the topic.

However, MRI scans show men use the left side of their brains for talking (O'Brien 2008). Before a man can discuss his feelings he must stop and think about how he feels (Coleman 2006), but a woman knows automatically. She can tell you how she feels, what she thinks, and what she believes all in a short, single sentence without pausing to breathe. A man pauses just to decide what he thinks.

Such brain differences become highlighted in the different behaviors of men and women. A woman enjoys talking because conversing activates the pleasure center of her brain, releasing the pleasure-producing hormone, oxytocin. If she feels an emotional disconnection that continues too long, she may begin an argument intentionally. For her, arguing is better than no connection when she needs an oxytocin charge.

A woman's release of oxytocin while talking is similar to the positive sensation she feels after crying. Watch a woman viewing a sad movie with a happy ending. After tearing, she feels happy and credits her positive mood to it being a great movie. She fails to realize that the release of oxytocin in her brain produces her pleasurable state, not the movie.

However, if a woman cries when she and her husband argue, often her husband feels repelled by her tears. Research that gathered women's tears and required men to smell them, found men lacked empathy for these women. In addition, men experienced a reduction in their testosterone level, the hormone associated with sexual arousal (Gelstein et al 2011). A woman tends to cry when she interprets her husband's comments as a personal affront, and often, her crying makes him defensive. He feels dumped on or manipulated; yet, her tears represent how painful she feels when emotionally estranged from him. A woman needs to assume responsibility for her emotions and express them in ways that draw her husband closer because when her husband responds with support, her mood experiences a dramatic improvement.

Why a Man Shuts Down

Unfortunately for women, MRI scans reveal that talking does little positive for a man. When a man speaks, he releases few pleasure-producing hormones. In fact, conversing can make a man feel worse. If the discussion turns negative, his brain fills with an unpleasant increase of cortisol that increases his stress level.

In addition, men find it difficult to talk deeply if they feel the slightest sense of shame as a provider, protector, lover, or parent (Stosney 2007). Shame represents a combination of disgrace, embarrassment, and inadequacy, and such feelings leave a man with a desire to hide.

John struggled with feelings of shame in all four areas. He experienced a debilitating sense of provider shame over having no income, and with Judy fearing they might become destitute his humiliation as a protector deepened. John admitted, "When Judy called me a loser, it ripped my gut. I felt like a loser already, and hearing her agree with my feelings proved more than I could handle. I wanted to die. I know she was angry, and we both say things we shouldn't when upset but lately it's been worse. My job loss seems to have brought out the worse in both of us. I wish I could protect her from worrying, but how can I with no job nibbles?"

John insisted they must cut all unnecessary spending. He hated telling the kids they could no longer see a movie, go to the water park, or eat out. He told their daughter she couldn't take the swimming lessons that he previously promised her. John questioned his ability as a provider, a protector, and a parent. Then when he and Judy argued, and she slept with the daughter, John felt a loser as a lover as Judy rejected being close to him. John felt overwhelmed with a powerful sense of shame. More than ever, Judy needed to supply his need for an abundance of the feel-good hormone oxytocin.

However, there remains another deeply seated reason why a man hates hearing his wife say, "We need to talk." Experience has taught him that she plans to bombard him with a long list of ways he should change. Her list causes him to feel inferior, as if he does nothing right, and he wants to run, not listen.

Eye Contact Is Often Difficult for Him

The topic discussed determines a man's desire for conversing. He enjoys talking while swapping factual information. Observe how comfortably men discuss cars, computers, and crises throughout the world. Men like discussing things while women prefer talking about people and their problems. A man keeps the focus off himself, but his private thoughts are the topic his wife enjoys discussing the most.

Many men talk more when they are not required to make direct eye contact for long periods of time during an emotional discussion. Research finds this trait begins in infancy. The more testosterone a child receives in the womb, the less eye contact the child makes by twelve months, and generally, a boy receives more testosterone than a girl (Lutchmaya, Baron-Cohen and Raggatt 2002). Women need to stop pressuring their men to look directly at them when a conversation turns heated. Men cannot do what their hormones won't allow them to do.

Increase His Feel-Good Hormones

Rarely, will intimate talking increase a man's comfort. However, the pleasure center of his brain does become activated with gentle physical touching by someone he likes or finds attractive (Amen 2009). He receives an oxytocin gratification with long hugs, kissing, hand holding, back rubs, and sex. A man craves physical touching and a woman cherishes long intimate talks because both like the feeling that an increase in oxytocin produces.

To help reduce John's discomfort with conversing, Judy agreed to hug John for several minutes before asking him to talk. He would be more receptive once his brain flooded with oxytocin, and his stress lowered. She encouraged John to take walks or go for drives and hold hands. This way John did not have to make direct eye contact for long periods. Such actions let both feel better connected, and they discussed minor issues with less drama.

Competition

A wife improves her marriage by realizing how competitive life is for her man. Remember men grow up competing and valuing being victorious: A date accepting his offer, having the best golf score, doing a good job, and being promoted. A man strives to win and come out on top. He lives hyper-sensitive to competition, especially to his wife's words that prove challenging. The first words a wife uses when beginning a discussion carry significant importance because they set the tone for what follows.

A wife benefits by first making a physical connection that lasts long enough to increase her husband's oxytocin level. Then, he responds better to her comments when they prove positive and nonthreatening. Instead of saying, "We need to talk," she can try, "Did you know. . ." Or, "Have you given any thought to. . ." Or, "I want your opinion about. . ." "Do you have any idea why. . .?" Such wording removes a man's fear of facing a stream of complaints. Questions force a man to think of an answer, instead of thinking about what might be coming next.

Increase Emotional Closeness for Him

When a woman shares long, intimate talks with her husband, she feels bonded, but he doesn't. A man does not require long discussions for connecting. He feels close when they share activities he finds enjoyable as Judy was about to learn. Sharing activities with his wife is one way a man intends to show her that he loves her.

Judy was fortunate to have parents who wanted to help when John lost his job. They recognized the tension Judy and John experienced. For Christmas, her parents gave them money for a weekend trip and offered to keep the children. Judy's mother wisely suggested they should do something John enjoyed.

Immediately, John chose rafting. He loved paddling rough waters but rarely mentioned it because their children were too young to go. With grandparents babysitting, the kids were no longer an issue. John asked to wait until spring in hope of having a job. He feared if they went now, he would feel guilty for not job-searching. Besides, by waiting, the weather would be warmer. He could think of nothing he would enjoy more.

"But, I don't think I will like rafting rough waters," Judy told her mother. "What if the boat overturns? I would hate it. The water would be freezing. I'd rather go someplace romantic. We have little of that anymore."

"You go to improve your relationship, not because you enjoy rafting," Judy's mother insisted. "A man likes sharing fun activities with the woman he loves. So go, and you won't regret it."

Reluctantly, Judy agreed. She promised not to let John know she hated the idea of rafting, but how she dreaded it.

In early spring, John and Judy rented a small cabin on the river. While rafting, their boat did capsize. After the initial shock of cold water soaking their bodies, they realized how humorous they must look to other boaters. They laughed all day about how silly they looked drenching wet and how water dripping down their backs felt like crawling bugs.

Later, snuggling by the fireplace, Judy understood why her mother insisted they share an activity John preferred. Judy fell asleep with her head lying in John's lap, while he continued talking. He shared ideas and plans and without her pressuring him. Relaxed and feeling close, John wanted to talk.

When you share a husband's favorite activity, he tends to talk all the way home. Feeling close removes pressure and fear for a man, and he discusses ideas that, he's kept to himself.

Whether your husband enjoys mountain climbing or biking, he likes having you along, provided you also find the activity enjoyable. He needs time alone and time with other men, but a husband likes knowing that his wife enjoys his favorite activities.

Because men enjoy sharing activities with their wives, some offer to take their wives shopping. They view it as a way of serving and giving her something she finds pleasurable. However, because he dislikes lingering in every department as she enjoys, often he suggests that he will wait in the car. Even when he tells her to take her time, it tends to ruin her shopping experience. She keeps reminding herself that she needs to rush because he is outside waiting. She cannot browse the entire store and enjoy the full, positive hormonal experience that shopping produces for females. But she can accept that he wanted to share time with her and chose an activity he knows she likes. For him, taking her shopping symbolizes sacrifice. The same sacrificial service holds true when he accompanies her to visit relatives he prefers avoiding.

His Comfort at Home

A man feels a sense of emotional attachment by being home with his family. After work, he shuts the door, forgets his day, and surrounds himself with those he loves. However if he experienced a bad day, he has no desire to relive the day verbally. He needs to unwind without discussing the day's details (Schulz et al 2004).

Remember God's punishment for Adam (and all husbands because they, too, sin) was that a man would painfully toil to make a living. God said, ". . . through painful toil you will eat" (Genesis 3:17). Once home, a man needs to forget work challenges. No matter how much he enjoys his chosen profession, he experiences a sense of relief to leave his job for a while.

However, some men have difficulty mentally shutting out job problems, especially if they left a task incomplete. In such cases, a wife can support her husband by giving him some downtime upon his arrival home. She can be present without talking, at least for a while. Quiet time is critical because research shows that unless he relaxes, his heightened emotional state causes his wife's stress level to also increase (Slatcher et al 2010). A wife needs to remember that even God valued a time of rest: "And on the seventh day God rested from all His work" (Hebrews 4:4).

In addition, men who fail to disengage from work tend to experience more health issues. They feel overly tired, have negative moods, and suffer sleep problems. Mark Cropley, author of "Switching off after Work" (Personnel Today 2010; personal correspondence 9/1/12), details that men have a three-fold increased risk of heart disease without adequate recovery from work-related stress. It remains critical for a man to view coming home as a time of being with a supportive spouse. Her greeting him with a warm hug increases his oxytocin level and lets her serve as his stress vaccine. A welcome home hug tells a man that she missed him, and a morning hug begins his day with good feelings about their marriage.

She needs to understand that a husband feels bonded just being home with her and the kids. He feels connected even if they are in another room. Closing the front door locks out the rest of the world, and he feels contented and secure, especially after a welcoming hug.

However, a man's need for some downtime after work is not implying a lack of interest in his wife's day. She should not interpret his quiet period as rejection. He just needs to unwind. While women find talking helps them de-stress, discussing job worries raises a man's stress level. A wife needs to give her husband some relaxation time and forego talks for an hour or so.

Men Like Routines.

Men value routines. While women tend to enjoy variety, most men prefer doing the same things in the same way. A routine allows a man to predict what might happen and have a ready response. His confidence grows by knowing in advance what he will do and how he will act. This reduces his fear of failing, facing disapproval, and feeling shame. Also, routines require less thinking, so he can become a little lazy.

For example, when John and Judy ate out, she preferred trying a new restaurant until they had eaten at all in town. Conversely, he wanted to go to the same Mexican restaurant. When asked why, he stated, "I know she really likes their veggie tacos. I know she will leave happy and won't complain about anything that happened there. I know I have chosen well."

Once a man finds what helps him feel comfortable, he likes to repeat it. He might claim, "I was this way when you married me. You had to know what to expect." Of course, he isn't. Like you, your husband changes frequently. He is not the same man you married. Likely, he's changed hobbies, tackled various recreational activities, expanded his waist size, increased his knowledge of many subjects, preferred newer cars, watched different TV programs, and parented differently with each additional child.

Becoming a Christian requires change. We strive to make choices that continue aligning closer to God's Word. Moving through the adult life cycle requires changing, some by choice and others by force. What a difference time makes.

A man repeats whatever he finds comfortable until a different challenge grabs his attention, someone shows him a better way, or another gives him no other choice, like when a wife files for divorce. Divorce proves especially difficult for a man because of how it disrupts his routine and removes his comfort zone. He no longer comes home after work to a family where he feels secure. Instead, he is left with fewer companions for sharing activities.

We Process Information Differently

Men and women think differently because they have unique experiences and because their brains produce differing amounts of hormones. According to Josh Coleman, author of *The Lazy Husband* (2006; personal correspondence 8/27/12), men and women moan, yell, cry, and laugh; however, they express these emotions differently. Men compartmentalize and intellectualize their feelings. Men often have to work to identify what they are feeling while women are more in touch with their emotions and feel freer to express them.

Men catalog each activity separately, but a woman's brain functions like a mass of interconnected wires. Each project a woman undertakes connects to her prior pursuit, and she is already planning another - or two. A woman's brain contains multiple networks that allow her to do several things simultaneously. The hippocampus, the center for learning, memory, and emotion, remains more active in women.

Men's brains have fewer connections. They function best when concentrating on one thing at a time because they tend to compartmentalize their thoughts. A man can focus intently for a long period, ignore distractions, and think only about the task at hand. (O'Brien 2008). However, if disrupted, he tends to become upset because he loses concentration. For example, suppose your man worked on taxes for an hour when you realize you needed to show him something. After your interruption, he may need to start over at the beginning. Only now he works annoyed.

Mark Gungor, creator of the program, *Laugh Your Way to a Better Marriage*, designed a humorous way for depicting male and female brain variations. He described a man's head as containing multiple boxes and depicted a woman's brain as a large mass of tangled, but connected, wires.

A husband uses a different mental box for processing information about each person and each activity in his life. He has a blue box labeled **TV**, another called **J** for his job, one marked with a **W** for his wife, one by each child's name, and one for each activity and each friend. His boxes rarely overlap.

Gungor emphasized men have one box marked with a large **E** that stands for Empty. If you attempt to talk with a man while he is in his Empty box, he will swear minutes later you never told him what you insist you did. The **E** box is the one in control while he flips TV channels. When you ask what he is watching, he says, "Nothing" because he genuinely means it. He remains unaware of what displays on the screen because he sits lost in his **E** box. He exercises his spastic thumb, while taking a brief mental nap with his eyes wide open.

However, a man's mental withdrawal does not imply escapism. Rather, he sits enjoying reprieve from daily stress, not retreat from his family.

During a man's resting state, his brain activity lowers significantly. Brain imaging scans reveals that a man's mind drifts when the task at hand requires little conscious attention. Brain scans taken during this mind-wandering state show the cortical regions of a man's brain remain active, but he remains unaware of what happens around him (Mason et al 2007).

By contrast, women never stop thinking. Their brains process information persistently. Brain scans reveal that a woman's brain during rest appears similar to a man's while he's performing a light mental task (Cheung as cited in Monroe 2009). A woman rarely experiences mental escapism. She remains mentally active, if not physically. She can wipe spilled milk off the floor, pull food from the freezer, and find a lost recipe, all without missing a beat while explaining a math problem for her child. Her head consists of pink connections, all wired together. Each wire carries a message which allows her to focus on multiple tasks simultaneously. Few men do that.

When a wife wants her husband to hear what she says, she must disrupt his mind-wandering state. Usually saying, "I have something I need to tell you," grabs his attention. To respond, he must switch from his **E**mpty box to his **W**ife box. Once she gains access, she ensures he remembers what she says by keeping her message brief - very brief.

When a woman's message runs too long, a man switches to another, more interesting box. He listens best when she sticks to basic, bare-bone facts. He waits for the most simple, essential content. He tunes out when her communication becomes a full-length story because he views too many details as useless and boring. Short and sweet is what works once she accesses his **W** box.

God did not wire the brains of men and women alike. Remember, Eve came from one of Adam's ribs, not his brain cells.

Judy never realized that a man thinks so differently. She admitted that, perhaps, some of the problems she and John experienced could be attributed to different hormones. She agreed to consider the idea. After learning why John seemed so withdrawn, she welcomed other ideas for reaching him. Sharing their canoe trip that ultimately proved a romantic get-away for Judy revealed a new way for her to communicate with John. She asked for other ideas for drawing them closer.

CHAPTER SEVEN

ADD SPICE IN YOUR SEX LIFE

"Sex, sex, sex. Is that all a man thinks about? Why can't a man care about what a woman likes? How can he want sex if we aren't feeling close?" Judy failed to recognize how satisfying John's sexual need would have him wanting to keep her happy outside the bedroom. She needed to know that research proves the more a man loves his wife, the more he desires sex with her (Schoenfeld, Bredow, and Huston 2013). How differently men and women think about sexuality and intimacy reveal one of their greatest brain differences.

A man's brain functions at a basic level when it comes to sex. His S box keeps sexual interest in a separate mental compartment, and it holds limited relation to emotions. For some men, sex can be just sex, with no connection to love. They can allow their physical urge to override emotions and even morals.

Sharing sexually creates a close emotional connection for a husband and he does not need to talk first. One of the rare times he meshes two mental boxes is during sex. His Sex and Wife boxes merge and unite completely. During sex, he receives his largest surge of oxytocin. He feels even better than a woman does after a long intimate discussion. Sex provides the ultimate boost of oxytocin.

But a woman rarely separates sex from feelings of intimacy. Sex for her implies she has a close relationship with her man. She tends to avoid a sexual encounter if she feels disconnected. Feelings control a woman's sexual desire, rather than thoughts about her husband's needs and God's commandments (1 Corinthians 7:3-5). When a woman becomes upset, she rejects sexual play until she again feels close. Her emotions need to stabilize first because relationship, sex, and feeling loved all intertwine inside a woman's brain. Therefore, frequent daily signs of affection elicit more sexual response from a woman than spur-of-the-moment suggestions, something many men fail to understand.

God Designed Sex

The Lord created us to desire sex, and a man's sexual alarm detects readiness 24/7. As his wife passes by, he may be unable to resist swatting her on the bottom, and then he's ready to race to bed. For him that swat represented foreplay. She may find this annoying at times, but he cannot help thinking about sex so often. Credit God, not him.

Research proves that exposing a man to sexually arousing stimuli causes his brain to release dopamine. With a dopamine surge, he not only becomes attracted to a pretty woman, he tends to want to pursue her. Then, testosterone focuses him on the physical part of sex (Kastleman 2007). During orgasm, a man releases testosterone, and his brain receives a huge surge of oxytocin (Moir and Jessel 1992). Once his body empties of testosterone, he commences another refill that eventually initiates another desire for release. His body simply responds like God created it to function.

A woman places a higher priority on relationships, and sex with her husband simply becomes another way for bonding. Even when a wife has no present desire, if she responds to her husband's advances, she can soon be in the mood. She feels better afterwards because she, too, receives a boost of oxytocin with an orgasm, and the increase is larger than she receives from talking.

However, some women rarely experience an orgasm. Being held, cuddled, and kissed, these women receive enough oxytocin to feel satisfied. Dianne Hales, author of *Just Like a Woman* (2000; personal correspondence 8/29/12), explains that a warm embrace and touch becomes these women's valued endpoint. They do not need an orgasm. Because a man's goal remains ejaculation, cuddling for him would never be this satisfying, and few understand how foreplay provides such satisfaction for a woman.

Danger of Mixed Priorities

Before some women think about sex, they want the children in bed and asleep, dishes in the dishwasher, the floor mopped, clothes folded and put away, all phone calls returned, and the grocery list completed. Then, she feels too exhausted to think about a romp in bed. Many women organize so many tasks they crowd sex from their thoughts and their time. Her multi-tasking confuses lesser important activities with the crucial importance of nurturing their sexual relationship. When a woman places sex at the bottom of her priority list, she misses the blessing the Lord designed for a couple. And she violates God's plan for their marriage. A husband needs assurance that he is more important to his wife than household chores.

When a wife asks to delay love making with the real intent of forgetting, or if she frequently meets her husband's invitation with "Not tonight" he receives her answer as rejection. However, "No," for a man is not simply a rejection of sex. A no represents a denial of his personal, masculine identity. Sex is essential for a man feeling loved and valued. If he suspects his wife cooperates only because she feels it a duty, he suffers immense humiliation. A stream of no's from his wife fosters deep resentment and alienation. Multiple no's confirm his deep fear that his wife finds him undesired as a lover, and he experiences the deepest possible sense of shame. Sexual acceptance digs deeply into a man's soul.

A husband who experiences frequent sexual rejection gradually loses desire for his wife. His pride wounds beyond repair. He hungers for physical pleasure but is unable to continue reaching for her. His ego cannot cope with continued rebuff. Because he feels betrayed, his wife should worry about another woman moving too close.

When He's Sexually Frustrated

God made sexual responsiveness a commandment for a reason (1 Corinthians 7:4). When a husband lives sexually frustrated and disappointed for an extended period, he cannot worship the Lord as he wants. Men and women control their sexual drives cognitively and hormonally. The part of a man's brain responsible for his sex drive is larger than a woman's and it causes him to think about sex more often (Brizendine 2011). When a man harbors a thwarted desire for sex, he does not think correctly. His frustrating thoughts override his rational thinking. He knows God placed the sexual desire in him but now his marriage is not functioning as God promised. He lives extremely frustrated. He feels alienated from the Lord and his wife is at least partially responsible. And she lives with God's disapproval.

Rejection creates such a deep hurt in a man, that Satan can use his pain and shame to tempt him to lust or even to commit adultery (1 Corinthians 7:5). God did not put such a strong desire in a man with the intention of him living a life of continued frustration.

A sexually distressed relationship needs immediate attention to live correctly with the Lord because sexually frustrated men often stop attending worship. Some seek spiritual counseling and say they no longer feel close to the Lord.

Rarely do they enter counseling admitting sexual frustration, and how it impacts their faith.

Our Bodies Belong to Our Spouses

The Lord meant for the sexuality of a married person to belong to the spouse. Scripture says the husband's body belongs to his wife and her body to her husband (1 Corinthians 7:4). Thus, refusing to sleep together as a way of punishing the spouse is sinful. Being angry and using separate sleeping arrangements as retaliation is quite different than briefly sleeping apart because of illness or making room for temporary guests.

God created our bodies to complement each other and blesses us with sex for keeping us close (Genesis 1:27, 28). Scripture includes a poetic textbook on sex in the Bible called Song of Songs. It describes physical and relational love and contains sensuous imagery about romance, passion, and privacy. God intends that a couple enjoy sex. Nothing a married couple shares exclusively together is wrong because sex is their spiritual wedding gift from the Lord.

If You Cannot Respond

If something genuinely bothers you and you need to postpone sex, be honest about why you hesitate and close your explanation with a promise that makes a delay worthwhile. Your husband will not view a postponement as rejection if coupled with assurance, "If we wait until morning I will make it worth the wait. I am very tired tonight and can respond better after resting." Keep your word. Upon waking, be the one to take the initiative because it was you who rescheduled with a commitment.

God says that sex is mandatory unless a couple agrees to a temporary delay in order to pray (1 Corinthians 7: 3-5). However in seminars, I confirm that every woman present has occasionally turned down her husband's advances. I have yet to find any woman who did so in order to pray. Women need to realize how connecting physically is as essential as connecting emotionally, and it remains more essential for a man. Both physical and emotional closeness create bonding in deep and fulfilling ways. God wired us differently to bring complete balance to the relationship. More often, she focuses on emotional closeness through verbal sharing; he contributes physical bonding with sexual pleasure.

If His Interest Slows

When deeply stressed, a man may lose interest in sex. If he lives fearing he might lose his job or a loved one is dying, he might not think about sex. During such times, if he says, "Not tonight," it does not imply that he no longer enjoys sex with his wife. He means, "Not until I feel better." Intense worry numbs the sexual libido for both genders. They should agree to delay sex and pray about the issue until the concern passes.

In addition, discord briefly inhibits a man's desire for sex. If a man feels belittled when he and his wife argue, he seeks distance, not closeness. However, he wants reconciliation once he compartmentalizes their conflicting differences and calms.

When his wife welcomes his attempt to reconnect, she regains the sense of closeness she lost during the conflict. However, when he wraps his arms around her, she often feels compelled to make one last defensive comment. She clings to a desire for him to understand how hurt she feels, but if she keeps her words kind and free of blame, he tends to remain close.

Having sex after quarrelling does not require an admission that either did something wrong. Instead, receptivity proves they love each other even when upset. Reconnecting confirms that a couple can strongly disagree and demonstrate that their relationship trumps a dividing issue.

Sexual Deterrents

Children can ruin any good sexual relationship. Their disruptive intrusions explain why some man invented locks for bedroom doors, and why parents need to insist that children go to bed nightly at a set time and in their own beds.

Before John lost his job, he and Judy reserved every Monday evening as a special sex night. They might have sex other times, but Monday remained a firm date night. They needed to reignite this lost passion, but first, they needed to reconnect in emotional ways. John's depression depleted his sexual drive and their lack of closeness affected Judy's esteem as she felt rejected.

They agreed to work on connecting closer. Judy greeted John with a long, lingering hug before breakfast, one every afternoon when he arrived home, and again as they prepared for bed. John wrote a one-line love message to Judy daily. He sent text messages, emails, and left an occasional hand-written note on her dresser. They shared long walks when the weather permitted, held hands, and talked about non-threatening issues. Such contact triggered hormonal rushes and increased their connection in ways each valued. John's love notes fed Judy's hunger for the attention she lost to his busy job search. Likewise, her physical touches increased John's positive hormonal release of oxytocin. Finally, they prepared to revive their prior sexual ritual.

On date nights, John stopped at a fast-food restaurant and bought dinner for the children. The children sat alone at the dining table, arranged with candles and cloth napkins. They thought it was their own special dinner when adults served them. Later, John heard about their day and listened to their prayers.

While John spent time with the kids, Judy prepared them a snack tray. The children were asleep by the time Judy and John ate, and they could retire to their room without fists pounding on their locked door. Reviving their special date night enhanced their closeness.

A couple's warm bonding carries over to their children. When they feel close to each other, their children feel secure. A couple should never use their children as an excuse for disobeying the Lord's command about meeting a partner's need for sex, or the partner is not the only one harmed.

Men Crave Eager Partners

The number one sexual complaint I hear when counseling men is how their wives do not respond aggressively in bed. When a wife reaches for her husband, he interprets her eagerness as meaning she finds him desirable and a good lover. A man's life glows when he feels desired sexually.

Husbands cherish spontaneous love-making as John Gray, author of *Women Are from Venus Men from Mars*, explains during speeches with this personal story. Dr. Gray's wife asked numerous times for him to take her to an opera. He created excuses because he dislikes such music. After days of her pleading, he decided to go, provided she would stop asking and agreed he only needed to attend this one time. He described sitting and praying for the music to end. Once they arrived home and parked inside the garage, his wife thanked him for taking her, pushed the button to close the garage door, and made love to him in the car. What impact did her sexually aggressive act of appreciation have? The following morning Dr. Gray slipped into his office and ordered them season tickets to the opera. Dr. Gray's response proved how a wife's occasional, spontaneous, aggressive act cemented their marriage in dramatic ways and how, afterwards, his wife reaped her desired emotional support.

You, too, can be sexually creative. The where and how is not relevant. What matters is that you take the initiative, so your husband knows you desire and want him. You are capable of making the sexual part of your relationship satisfy all your husband's dreams.

Make Sex Fun

During seminars, I ask women to make a list of things they could do to make sex be more fun for their husbands. Sadly, instead, their list describes things that create a romantic setting for themselves. They suggest playing soft music, lighting candles, and spraying pillows with cologne.

For women the environment proves important, but that's less essential for him. It is the same when they eat out. She likes candlelight, cloth napkins, and background music. He thinks about the food's quality, available choices, and cost.

Women become aroused by romantic words and soft music because their fantasies include romance and commitment. Helen Fisher, author of *First Sex* (2000), explains that women place intercourse within the wider context of the relationship due to their brain architecture and the way they see the world (personal correspondence 9/17/12). Intercourse for a woman implies that she carries within her heart an emotional bond with her partner.

A man does not crave romantic settings. In fact, some men complain of finding it unromantic when their wives light candles. These men prefer additional lighting because a man's predominant perceptual sense is vision, and they are more visual than women (Fisher 2000). Research requiring men and women to watch identical sexual stimuli reveals the emotional center of the brain, the amygdala and hypothalamus, activates more strongly in men when watching sexual images (Hamann et al 2004). Because a man's brain experiences a stronger reaction to sexual images, women need to consider how they dress and prepare a bedroom. They need to accept that his desires differ from hers and commit to satisfying the needs God placed in him.

After learning what pleased a man, Judy promised to make sex more exciting for John, and she did a great job. Without telling him, Judy left the kids with grandparents. When John pulled into the driveway, she turned off all the lights and lit candles that led his way to the bathroom. A handwritten note lay beside each candle that instructed John to remove a piece of his clothing. When he arrived in the bathroom with nothing on, he found Judy inviting him to join her in a tub of warm bubbles.

When John traveled overnight for job interviews, Judy pinned a note to the inside of his undershorts saying she wished she was there. She hid notes inside his billfold and shirt pockets, saying she missed him and would show him how much when he returned home. Judy proved how sexually creative a woman can be, and her actions told John how she valued him as a lover.

Maximize the After-glow Period

According to research, a couple can stay awake longer following intercourse if they take deep breaths during orgasm, rather than holding their breath (Brizendine, 2011). Neither feels as exhausted, and they experience the afterglow period longer. Women, especially, enjoy this time because a man tends to listen better after sharing sex with a responsive wife. His brain receives an abundant surge of oxytocin and vasopressin. These hormones generate bonding and trust and reduce his fears and inhibitions; thus, it creates a ripe time for satisfying her emotional cravings. The large boost of oxytocin lasts as long as two days for some women. However for a man, once his body begins making testosterone again, his oxytocin effect starts dissipating and may be diminished completely after a couple of hours (Love 2007, 2011).

The afterglow period can serve as an ideal time for praying about issues that prove difficult to discuss, provided you do so before your man's brain chemicals cause him to fall asleep. Remember, during orgasm, a man fills with the trusting and bonding chemicals and his inhibitions lessen, so he listens more with his heart than his head. He can listen if you share aloud your deepest desires, hurts, and joys with the Lord.

When you share your most closely guarded, private concerns with God in your spouse's hearing, at first, you may feel awkward and uncomfortable. However, after several times, you feel bonded physically, emotionally, spiritually, and mentally. When you become transparent to the very core of your being, you eliminate sinful toxins from your heart and leave space for the Lord to develop a greater oneness in your marriage. What other time can you connect so completely?

However, do not expect your husband to participate until you have prayed numerous times. Remember sharing aloud your most guarded concerns seems awkward, and men hate feeling vulnerable. Give him time to become comfortable with your prayers and at some point, he may join you. Do not pressure him. Just continue praying. Even if he never joins in, remember, you do not require his participation. You are talking to God, not your husband.

Dangers of Oxytocin Boosts

I would be remiss not to mention a danger of having sex with someone outside of marriage because of how good oxytocin makes one feel. Many people mistakenly credit their positive hormonal feeling to being in love with their sexual partner (Love 2007). Thus, parents have an additional reason for encouraging their children to postpone sex until marriage. Otherwise, they may credit the intensely good feeling to their partner and marry a person who is not a good match or even good marriage material. Research shows women are very vulnerable to mistaking love for good feelings following sex. The oxytocin rush has them making a wrong connection between sexual pleasure and love of their partner (Diamond 2004).

Perhaps, mistaking an oxytocin rush for love may help explain why some women find abusive men attractive. She feels great after sex with him, credits him for such positive emotions, and thinks she loves him. Because she feels good, she minimizes his cruel behaviors. However, an oxytocin increase is not necessarily an indication of love. It is just a hormonal surge making her feel good. Treatment outside the bedroom counts the most when choosing a marriage partner.

We must remember that God condemns sex outside of marriage (1 Corinthians 6: 18-20), and if we deliberately rebel against His laws, God does not promise us heaven. Fortunately, He does promise forgiveness with repentance, and He will then help us find someone well-suited for marriage.

Respect Your Husband's Desire

The more you respond sexually to your husband, the better respected he feels as a lover. The more esteemed your husband feels, the more he wants to meet your needs.

I assured Judy that once she appreciated John's sexual needs, they would become as connected outside the bedroom as inside. She committed to being an active sexual partner, but stressed that they needed to learn to communicate about disturbing issues without anger and hurt. Otherwise, they rarely felt loving. It seemed appropriate to understand their fight-flight pattern next

CHAPTER EIGHT

FOUR DISCONNECTS

When you are arguing with your husband, Jesus stands beside you pleading, "Woman, stop. Hush, woman. Woman, stop using those words." However, while angry, a wife rarely ends her complaining. She tends to continue until her husband becomes heated, and they disconnect emotionally. More often it's her that initiates such a discussion. We know this from research conducted with hundreds of long-term married couples that finds wives begin the majority of arguments (Gottman 1999).

Practically, all of Judy's and John's disagreements centered on their children or money. John, being more of a conflict avoider, tended to make rules and break them which annoyed Judy the enforcer of order. He tended to take things in stride and his delay caused Judy to panic because she wanted things done and over with. However, when it came to chores for the kids, John held them accountable for tasks they were old enough to handle, and Judy wanted to pamper and keep them dependent on her. Neither style was right or wrong – they just different. Yet, because both wanted to be right, it meant they strove to override the other.

Frustrated, a woman wants to talk about their problem - and right now. Because she feels overloaded with emotions, she ignores that she uses a sharp tone and curt words. She may raise her voice, as if doing so will ensure he listens. But even when she raises her tone only slightly, her words hurt, and he hears them as a megaphone slammed against his ear. He reacts by being silent, unless he feels backed into a corner. Then he counterattacks vigorously before leaving. He takes flight by sitting stone-faced in dead silence or by leaving physically. Either way, he detaches and becomes emotionally absent.

This pattern appeared typical of John's and Judy's fights. When asked to describe their arguments, John related, "Usually, I am feeling fine, busy doing my thing, and without notice Judy blasts me with accusations of things I don't even remember. I have no idea why she is so upset, but I know we face a longer battle if I say anything. It seems safer to leave than to argue and risk saying something that upsets her more. I leave, hoping it will blow over sooner." John did not believe he could calm Judy's frustrations by talking.

Judy blamed John for their disagreements. "He never finishes an argument. He walks away and leaves things hanging. When he returns, he wants to make-up but without talking about the problem." Judy needed to understand why her approaches for reaching John failed and learn alternatives to pull him closer.

Four Big Disconnects

There are four ways that women like Judy rupture their marriages when feeling needy. I call these the four big disconnects: (1) By criticizing their husbands; (2) trying to force husbands to change; (3) insisting husbands accept their reasoning; and (4) bringing up a topic in a way that initiates an argument. All four leave a lasting negative effect on their relationships. These four tempt men to choose flight and fight, not closeness. When a man feels attacked or shamed, he wants to flee and duck for cover, not discuss an issue. He does not listen. He cannot listen. The more injured a man feels the tighter his lips lock. He cannot respond lovingly while nursing a festering wound.

Why Criticism Fails

When we behave in ways the Lord condemns, we eventually fail. Paul tells us, "Do everything without complaining or arguing" (Philippians 2:14). James warns not to grumble against each other, or "you will be judged" (James 5:9), and "If anyone considers himself religious and does not keep a tight rein on his tongue, he deceives himself, and his religion is worthless." (James 1:26). God condemns such speech because of how our spouses feel and react when we say something that leaves them degraded.

Few people change or fully cooperate because of criticism. If they did, our world would contain only perfect people because who hasn't been criticized? Critical comments produce change when such remarks shame the person. However, the person tends to change to avoid future humiliation and forgets feeling belittled or degraded. Receptivity requires a genuinely open heart, and few of us meet the test regardless of how accurate or helpful the criticism.

Even if a wife apologizes following her critical comments and admits she regrets what she said, a painful sting remains. Her husband may say, "Forget it. It is okay," but believe me, it isn't. Some resentment lingers.

However, acknowledging hurt feelings does not harm the relationship. Damage occurs when words intended to describe the hurt shift to attacks and negative labels.

Asking for Change Fails

Judy needed to exercise equal caution when she asked John to make a change. She needed to ensure her requests did not imply he was a failure. John felt devastated already over his boss' message. He could not cope with a painful confrontation from Judy too. His ego remained as fragile as hers.

When a woman expresses her wishes in demeaning ways she creates serious problems. She believes she is telling her husband precisely what she needs him to do differently. But when he ignores her request, she often attempts to force him to obey. Unfortunately, she rarely admits that she seeks obedience. Instead, she tells herself she wants him to care about her discomfort. With his continued noncompliance, she becomes incensed, barks harsh words, and ups her pressure. When she increases her fight attacks, her husband moves even farther away emotionally, and she condemns him for distancing. She rarely admits to her use of force or desire to control.

A husband despises it when his wife attempts to boss and force him to change. Her use of pressure implies that her idea of how something should be handled remains superior to his. A man lives hyper-sensitively to role status and becomes intolerant of words that leave him feeling inferior. Research finds men converse to try and win debates and communicate in one-up-man-ship (Furumo and Pearson 2007). Taking orders from his wife causes him to experience a severe loss of independence and a fear that he holds a lowered position in their relationship. He responds by trying to save face. Pride becomes central, as he resists any influence. A man will not tolerate feeling less, regardless of how right his wife may be.

A wife with an unresolved issue tends to become a complainer and nags from the minute her husband arrives home until he leaves again. She may even phone and send critical emails to his workplace. She applies a negative interpretation to everything he says and fails to consider what would have him cooperating and what adjustments this requires of her. Sadly, it may be that he knows such a change would improve their marriage, but the approach she uses has him stubbornly protecting his stance. His pride reigns. However, if she altered her style, he would more likely respond. She needs to stay focused on her goal, not his reaction. Unless, of course, being in control is her goal.

Problem with Trying to Reason

Judy and John lost a sense of closeness with the tiniest amount of bitterness. When he withdrew, she retreated, too, in fear of more pain. Flight increased pain for both of them. Although Judy withdrew and sulked, eventually she could tolerate isolation no longer and attempted to reason with John. She hoped her argument would convince him to view things her way. She believed she had a solid reason for feeling upset and hoped John would care if he just understood.

Only John could not listen. Judy's reasoning implied that his rationale was flawed, inferior, and wrong. Only if John remained calm enough to listen would rational logic penetrate his heart, and Judy's insistence that he was at fault never produced calmness. Both acted like selfish children and continued arguing. Judy needed to change how she approached John if she hoped to gain his cooperation.

Initiating Anger

When either party begins a discussion that has the spouse feeling attacked, both lose. All listening stops. Rather than hearing the intent of the speaker, the listening spouse forms a defense to protect self and speaks in ways that sound like a counter-attack. Both feel hurt and self-protect, rather than working to solve the issue. They raise their voices as if loudness forces the other to hear. Ultimately, one withdraws. Nothing's resolved, and feelings remain raw. They must learn to approach the other using words that open the spouse's ears and heart.

CHAPTER NINE

HOW ANGER SWELLS

Judy agreed to record their next heated dispute because, like many women, she tended to be the one who started their quarrels. Recorded words would let us work together to identify ways Judy and John fostered anger. I encouraged Judy to leave the recorder playing and express her inner thoughts aloud, even if John left the house. What Judy typically said to herself during John's absence could indicate areas where altering her self-talk might help.

However, once John left, the machine went silent, but both seemed receptive to sharing what they thought during their time apart. Listening to how they sounded when angry in the presence of an outsider made a dramatic impact on their self-esteem. No longer could they deny how rudely they spoke to each other.

If anything induces a spouse to change how they talk when upset, having an outsider hear them does. God instilled shame and guilt in us because they stir our soul with passion for repentance and forgiveness, and Judy and John needed to repent for how they treated each other – and change.

How Anger Progresses

Disagreements occur when something we want becomes blocked. For example, Judy valued having something, and

John prevented her attainment because her goal conflicted with what he wanted. He held no intention of causing her discomfort or withholding what she wanted. He concentrated on his own activity and neglected to consider Judy's wishes, why she wanted it, or how she felt. Neither meant to cause the other hurt nor frustration.

As typical, Judy's comments initiated this chain of retorts. She interrupted John's thoughts with a tone that raked his nerves, but she meant no disrespect. "I wish you could stop long enough to listen, because I have something that needs your attention. I know you'd rather not, but I need help." Her stress drove her pitch, not anything John did. She spoke insensitively, and John looked up with a stone-faced glare.

John, absorbed in his own thoughts, found Judy's interruption annoying. It challenged his comfort. He admitted thinking, *"Judy could speak kindly, but instead, she acts like her usual self."* John became upset more by what he told himself than by Judy's words. He could have provided Judy an acceptable excuse for why she spoke rudely, but, instead, John returned an aggressive comment. "If you can't speak nicely, then hush. Didn't your mother teach you that it's better to be quiet than to speak rudely? So, please, just hush."

"I'm not the one being mean. You are." Judy felt hurt and snapped back. Both could take a deep breath and think about how they sounded. Instead, both chose self-protection. They charged ahead, prepared to defend their stance. They spoke hoping to prove their point, but they made no impact because their choice of words and tones wounded the other.

"Judy, please, just hush. The more you say, the worse things get and you know it." John wanted to change the subject, but it proved too late.

Judy wasn't about to be told how to behave. Such a command increased her desire for self-protection. Instead, she could have asked if she said something wrong and allowed John to explain how her words affected him. But she was not about to let him tell her how she should conduct herself.

Finally, John's tolerance level peaked. He made one last offensive comment, "Why can't you just talk like a normal person? Why do you always have to begin every talk by attacking me? Do you really think the way you speak makes me want to help you?" He raced out the door convinced that nothing could be gained by staying. John wanted to be far away from Judy's aggressive remarks and out of hearing range of their children.

Unspoken Rules

Like most couples, John and Judy function with their own private, unspoken set of rules. Rules serve to support our valued beliefs and help us avoid fearful circumstances. They intend to ensure every situation flows according to how we want others to treat us.

Unfortunately, people attempt to enforce their rules without others knowing the standards. Rarely does a person say, "I carry this rule in my head that says a husband always . . ." "My internalized rule is that a wife should never . . ." They operate with two types of rules: Moral-based rules, laws they believe God requires, and personal preference rules designed for obtaining personal desires.

We assume if another breaks our rule, we will experience hurt. We believe the entire world finds our rules worthy and that everyone desires the same. Unfortunately, personal preference rules represent expectations for how we want others to behave. Rarely do they direct our own conduct.

When John felt a sting of annoyance, he looked to Judy to determine why he felt uneasy. He never considered that he could have misinterpreted her remarks. Judy broke one of his rules, and it left him feeling justified in being angry. "Judy did it again. Why can't she speak nicely to me?" He ignored that he could have told Judy, "Such a loud tone hurt because I felt scolded, but I don't think you meant it that way. I want us to begin again. I do not want to snap back and hurt you too."

The times that Judy spoke kindly to John she protected his personal preference rule. He felt loved and adored her, but when she spoke in ways that upset him, John experienced a strong dislike for her. He wanted to run away and avoid all contact with her. Likewise, Judy underwent a similar mental process judging John's conduct against her rules and treated him in unkind ways when he broke her rules.

Judging Another's Behavior vs Our Intent

Our sinful nature lets us minimize our own wrongs and magnify other's faults. We treat ourselves with compassion and sympathy and rarely acknowledge our own negative character traits. At least, not until things cool. Thus, what begins as an annoyance quickly escalates to anger and our sins multiply. Our words and actions should repulse us and create an immediate desire to ask forgiveness, but they rarely do.

During this argument, Judy evaluated her own behavior by what she hoped to accomplish when she spoke to John. She wanted John's assistance for help with the children. She held a good intent. Therefore, her personal self-evaluation remained positive. However, she rated John's actions by how she felt after he broke her rule by rudely telling her to hush. Her emotions reigned. Her rule required a husband to ask what she meant before over-reacting.

Other Intended Hurt

Judy and John felt offended with their rules broken. Under typical conditions, they ignored when the other responded abruptly. However, with their stress peaked at an injurious level, the slightest mistake by the other appeared catastrophic. They believed every word the other said carried abuse and insisted it was intended to inflict pain. They exchanged insult for insult. Both focused on the other's sins and failed to acknowledge their own.

At any time, both could question, "Is this how I want to be acting?" Asking would challenge them to change. But it is easier to look externally than at self.

Judy insisted, "John knows that telling someone to hush hurts. He just didn't care."

Search for Additional Evidence

When our defense proves too weak to stand on its own, we seek proof from other sources and examples from the past that bolster our case. We dramatize other incidents or call on others, as if an increase in numbers makes our wrong appear right.

After John withdrew, Judy dissected her memory searching for additional times when he behaved in non-caring ways. To magnify her stance, she tagged on times she thought John treated others wrongly. Her resentment grew as she questioned, "Who wouldn't be upset after such mistreatment? I know he sure hurt mother last month when he snapped at her for waking one of the children. This is the last straw. John behaved like this last month, last Christmas, and even on our honeymoon."

Other choices remained for Judy. She could tell herself, "I am upset and angry, but John has many good qualities I like, especially his . . .".

Anger Hides Fears

Anger camouflages esteem fears. Ego fears concentrate on feeling disrespected and disregarded, such as looking dumb, fearing rejection, doubting love, losing control, feeling used, or believing another cheated us. Esteem fears often override moral values and allow us to ignore how we sin.

When John ignored Judy's original request, she expressed anger instead of examining what she feared might happen if John ignored her appeal. The stronger her fear, the less validity her perspective held. She exaggerated each detail. Every thought became negative, and she dismissed all of John's good qualities, the things that attract her to him.

Judy and John can learn to question what fears drive their anger and share this fear with each other. However, it takes desire and practice to refrain from arguing long enough to identify the fear.

Justifying Blame

When we feel irate, there's a strong need to determine what caused others to treat us as they did. Adjectives and adverbs dominate our vocabulary to prove that the other is fully at fault. Our anger turns to contempt once we blame the other completely. Once sin takes hold, it escalates.

Judy insisted that John's behavior remained their problem. Because she knew she meant well, their current conflict belonged exclusively to him. She insisted that John's sinful attributes of selfishness, spitefulness, and self-centeredness created the issue and such attributes also received the Lord's disapproval. Judy reinforced her personal preference rule with a moral value rule to make John's behavior appear worse.

However, no matter how Judy tried to convince herself that John remained completely at fault, she knew better. While John acted selfishly and self-centeredly at times, he doesn't all the time, and she, too, had selfish moments that needed forgiveness.

Other Acts Immoral

Rarely do we realize that we are judging and playing the role of God. We pretend that we know exactly why others behave as they do. We convince ourselves that the other's sinfulness causes the problem and none belongs to us. Self-love and pride prejudice us for condoning our own wrongs, while condemning others; yet, deep within our hearts, we know the truth.

In Judy's mind, John was no longer guilty of having broken a personal preference rule. He committed an immoral act, and she believed God agreed with her. Making the problem into a moral issue let Judy safeguard a sense of self-respect. Labeling John with negative adjectives, she felt less vulnerable. As Judy thought about what happened and how wrong John behaved, she became irate.

I'm Good to Him; He's Mean to Me

While upset, we rarely condemn ourselves. Instead, we enhance positive descriptions of ourselves. If we cannot make ourselves look good, we make ourselves appear innocent. We expend tremendous energy to force our conscience to conform to our behavior, rather than making our thoughts, words, and actions conform to our conscience. We commit the same sins as another and excuse ourselves while condemning the other (Romans 2:1). Every man's way seems right in his own eyes (Proverbs 21:2).

While emotional, we never stop and count the number of wrongs we commit. Self-reflection and self-assessment should push us to our knees to plead for forgiveness, but, instead, pride rules. We value feeling good about self above all else.

Infuriated, Judy measured her good deeds against John's failures. She reassured herself that she would never behave towards him as he treated her. Her thoughts dwelt on all the good things she did for John and how little she received in return. She compared his behavior against her good intentions and forgot that her original comment triggered their conflict.

The longer Judy's list of her own good actions and memories of John acting rudely, the more victimized she felt. If she recalled a time when she hurt John, she minimized its impact so she could consider herself innocent. Now that Judy felt victimized, she prepared to pulverize John.

Revenge Ready

Retaliation seems justified once a victim mentality occurs. Dwelling exclusively on feelings of mistreatment, we become insensitive to our impulse for punishing the other. The harder we focus on how the other mistreated us, the easier it is to design ways for getting even. Refusing to act on revenge feelings requires tremendous self-control. The only escape from such a doomed outcome is self-examination of our own wrongs, and that requires a genuine humbleness we don't have at this point.

Judy felt justified in desiring revenge. She numbed her conscience by repetitively emphasizing her victimization. She tended to first use fight and verbally assault John when he returned. Then, she shifted to flight by refusing to speak and sleeping with their daughter several nights. Eventually, she could no longer tolerate isolation and spoke using milder fight words, but her comments still ensured that John knew she seethed with continued anger.

You Over-reacted

At this stage, Judy and John cared only about proving self right and the other wrong. Judy ignored how she had yet to tell John what she wanted that initiated their estrangement.

Both thought the other over-reacted. John doesn't believe how he responded to Judy's crude comment was as bad as she claimed. Both think the other demonstrated an exaggerated reaction to their insignificant behavior. They questioned why the other acted rudely and lost all sensitivity for the other's pain.

Shredded Trust

John's and Judy's pain should be cooled by now, but instead, both felt rotten because they sacrificed a sense of personal esteem. They disliked each other. They also felt ashamed for how they continued behaving. However, by now it required an outsider to have them admit it. Their pride controlled and supported estrangement.

With trust now shattered, they isolated themselves. Judy hid in her children's activities and John in mailing resumes. Both put energy into self-protection. They supported the rift by ignoring how the chain of events could be halted. They both used withdrawal for punishing the other.

Men Bury in Activities; Women Gossip

John filled his mailbox with resumes and sent them to places he knew were useless, but it occupied his time. He withdrew more and more into his Empty box and comforted himself in mindless TV programs.

Judy sought support elsewhere. No longer able to bottle her feelings, she phoned her sister, Jan, and shared her sorrowful story in hopes of receiving sympathy and approval. By turning to Jan to discern right and wrong, instead of the Lord, Judy risked hardening her conscience more.

Judy knew Jan could not resolve the issue, but she did not care. She craved emotional support. Judy wanted to hear that she had not behaved so badly and had good reasons for how she felt. Pacifying her feelings, out-ranked doing what's right for her marriage.

However, Judy was not completely open and honest. She omitted several facts. She excluded how she allowed the issue to escalate without any attempt at resolution and how she, too, spoke hateful words. She did not admit how she still had not told John what she originally wanted, the most commonly omitted part of any argument.

Telling Jan let Judy avoid the tension associated with confronting John in a loving way for resolving the matter and being close again. Worse, she risked developing a habit of blaming another for the discomfort in her life and searching for help from others who should not know such private matters.

Judy ignored that telling Jan about the discord had her gossiping, and how devastated John would feel when he learned Jan knew intimate details. John would have trouble facing Jan again and remember forever that Judy shared personal information.

Children's Needs Go Unheeded

While arguing, a couple bestows affection on no one, including their small children. A child may crawl into one of their laps, but even young ones know when they do not receive full attention.

John and Judy ignored their children's need for comfort in such a tense environment because their own pain absorbed their every thought. In addition, what they taught the children about handling differences impeded their children's healthy development.

Plank in Own Eyes

Judy's and John's example of how anger progresses demonstrates why Scripture says, "In your anger, do not sin" (Ephesians 6:26). For fight – flight couples, marital anger remains one of the most difficult sins to conquer. Once a couple interprets their partner's words as intending to inflict hurt, they shift into a self-protection mode and judge the other's motive as bad. They ignore how it may simply reflect what Jesus called a speck in the other's eye while having a large plank in one's own eye (Matthew 7:4). They judge themselves as if they behaved beyond judgment or fault. Yet, in reality, they have no idea of the other's motive or intention. This explains why Jesus calls them to clean their own thoughts, feelings, words, and actions before attempting to correct the other (Matthew 7:5).

Jesus demands self-examination first, because introspection forces us to admit our wrongs and seek forgiveness from both the Lord and our spouse. Then our arguments remain a simple disagreement, rather than developing into a full-scale war. Prayer stifles the ego's demand to put self-pride above another's feelings and stops the embellishment of hurt. With prayer, the relationship heals.

However, the longer an attack-avoid couple go without attempting to reconnect, the more fragile the relationship becomes. Because resentment lies at the root of divorce, these couples live in grave danger. When one threatens divorce, the other either agrees, "Do it! Go for it! I should have left you long ago," using words that drive hurt deeper. Or the person feels like an explosion has occurred in the head and freezes, unable to talk or cope. And to think such an outcome often began with a thoughtless, critical sounding comment said in hopes of having the spouse act more loving. When such disintegration causes either partner to threaten divorce, Satan controls their relationship, their home. And it's all due to the fact that our normal behavior stance has become self-protection, instead of loving, serving, and respecting the other.

When Satan Reigns

Sadly, the divorce rate ranks almost as high among Christian believers as nonbelievers, and it is particularly true for couples who only sporadically attend worship services (Barrick 2008). Divorcing couples failed to make a commitment of never using the D word, regardless of how upset they became.

Arguing allows Satan to gain a foothold in our relationships. He blinds us to our own faults and has us believing we act better than we do. He targets our conscience to harden it, so we will ignore and dismiss the truth about how wretched we often behave.

Choosing a fight - flight reaction and entrapping a couple's thoughts with ideas of divorce excites Satan because he knows God's hurt again. Sadly, John's and Judy's hostile arguments terrified their helpless, innocent children, and that surely thrilled Satan even more.

Divorce Impacts Many

Malachi (2:13-16) explains that the Lord hates divorce. No matter how reasonably a divorce ends, violence harms every person involved. Typically, divorce floods a couple with guilt and makes them vulnerable to emotional decay. They often experience depression, and many harbor a lingering desire for revenge. Worse, many stop attending worship; yet, research proves that faithful attendance at worship services increases one's overall wellbeing (Mochon, Norton, and Ariely 2007). After failing in a marital relationship, the couple finds it easier to leave each succeeding marriage. Flight becomes an internalized, accepted pattern, but God's goal for us remains peaceful unity, not separation.

The Lord says He makes a married couple one in flesh and spirit because He seeks godly offspring (Malachi 2:15). Divorce often finds the couple's children withdrawing from the Lord as they pray for the Lord to save their families and parents won't listen. In addition, parental divorce programs the involved children to fail in their own marriages, if they even wed. Many do not. In *Understanding the Divorce Cycle: The Children of Divorce in Their Own Marriages* (2005), Nicholas Wolfinger details how divorce creates ripe circumstances for the children to experience more issues than just behavioral and health problems. They make poor partner selections and face serious problems in their own marriages.

Some children turn away from the Lord, and their withdrawal causes them to miss the Lord's comfort today and heaven later.

Pain of divorce extends beyond the immediate family. Ask any parent whose child divorces. Their life suffers great loss. Even friends experience sadness and emptiness when their relationships must be reshaped. Divorce remains a community concern.

Prayer is mandatory because it allows God to heal all wounds. When a couple will turn to Him before bringing up a sensitive topic, God promises to help us defeat Satan's attacks (1 Corinthians 10:13). When a couple prays, He fills both hearts with the loving desire to serve each other. Marriages experience a dynamic improvement, when both parties surrender self-wills to God's will because hurtful words do not just rip their hearts, such words tear deeply into their souls in ways that only the Lord can heal.

The Lord intends for us to learn to love the ones we marry. Our decision to remain committed to the spouses we married, regardless of how annoying they may appear at times, creates the greatest marital happiness. Such a commitment forces us to develop an attitude of, "Our relationship is more important than this issue." Keeping the relationship above all problems teaches us how to keep covenant promises for a lifetime.

How We Disagree Matters

Judy and John had to make changes for improving their marriage, to live in right relationship with the Lord, and to protect their children. They needed to quit telling themselves the other intends to inflict hurt and replace such thinking with actions and words that affirmed trust and love.

To change, Judy and John required recognition of their fight pattern. Because they misinterpreted the other's words and behaviors, they disconnected and often for days. Both craved reassurance that the other cared and hated it when they inflicted hurt.

John's and Judy's misinterpretations triggered their fear of not being loved and respected, and their immediate reaction was to self-protect. Their attitudes became, "If you won't care for me, I will do it myself, and the only way I can protect me from your hurt is to push you away." Yet, what they hoped to achieve was, "Love me more. Be there for me because I am hurting. I feel disconnected and want to feel close with you."

As a man feeling disconnected, John tackled an activity to distract and hide his feelings of guilt. He withdrew from the relationship to hide in his mental man cave and calm his feelings of shame. Judy, as a typical woman with a strong craving for closeness and protection, sought a connection with another so she could again feel cared for and valued. Feeling abandoned, she turned to her sister who defended her.

When they are connected, a couple can communicate about any topic. Without connection, their communication always turns into an argument.

The only way for John and Judy to reconnect was not to communicate about what happened, because too often this type of discussion created additional arguing. Rather, feeling close again required forgiveness that only results from confession, repentance and deep heart-felt remorse of their wrong behaviors.

Still, Judy and John possessed numerous positive qualities. They learned early in their marriage to laugh as much, if not more, than they disagreed. They tended to express joy and happiness to the same degree they tolerated negativity. Even their children described them as fun parents.

Marital problems remain more serious when one partner avoids differences and the other consistently presses to discuss them, but this definitely did not describe Judy and

John. At least as a couple, they appeared emotionally balanced. They both wanted to discuss their problems. They just let emotions take hold of how they spoke. They were often rationally right but emotionally wrong. Unfortunately, only when they stay emotionally connected can either care about rational ideas.

The problem is not that Judy and John disagreed. Disagreeing ensured that they discussed issues rather than letting them simmer and multiply. How they addressed their different ideas was what needed altering and that required learning to control their emotions. They also needed to learn to repair any lingering pain.

Judy wanted to know how to reduce John's desire to leave the house when he became upset. Doing so, would decrease her fear of abandonment. But the first task for John and Judy was to make amends and forgive because their current relationship remained fragile. Fortunately, they both possessed a strong desire to make-up..

CHAPTER TEN

PROBLEMS WITH FORGIVING

"**A**fter an argument, I always regret how I acted," Judy admitted. "But I am hurting so deeply that I can't handle it. It's like I can't cope. I need John to comfort me, and he leaves when I need him the most. Later, I tell him I am sorry, but then something else happens, and I react the same way."

Judy regretted how she behaved, but she couldn't seem to stop. I explained that it's like the thief who regrets being caught and is embarrassed because others know. But when faced with temptation again, he steals without thinking of the consequences.

Change requires repentance, and true repentance requires genuine, deep sorrow for the hurt and disappointment we caused another and the Lord. Repentance runs deeper than simply being embarrassed because feeling ashamed has us thinking about our own feelings, rather than the feelings of the ones we harmed. Genuine sorrow focuses on how hurt the other is and also how grieved the Lord feels. When we injure another, we also pain the Lord. The Lord takes how we treat others very personal (Acts 22:6; Exodus 16:7,8).

Such harm is a form of betrayal and explains why Peter wept so after he denied knowing Jesus. Peter pledged faithfulness but at the moment he was challenged, he thought only about self-protection, not how his denial would hurt Jesus. Without genuine remorse, like Peter expressed later, change is rarely permanent. We may apologize but without emotional sorrow, our actions rarely support our words, at least not consistently.

Neither Judy nor John realized that each time they attacked the other, they also hurt the Lord. Realizing the number of times they pained God provided additional motivation for them to change.

When men and women become so upset they no longer function comfortably, they react differently. Men tend to attack and flee because being alone lets him compartmentalize the issue inside his thoughts. Once calm, he dismisses what happened. Few men dwell days or weeks on what happened. However, the incident for a woman remains far from resolved. She ruminates days, weeks, sometimes years.

Women's Painful Memories

God instructs, "Do not let the sun go down while you are still angry" (Ephesians 4:26). God emphasizes the danger of a lengthy estrangement, partly because of what a time delay does to a woman. MRI scans of women's brains show that when a woman experiences a strong, negative episode her brain overlaps the recording of the event in areas that store both memory and emotions (Kensinger 2007). Because her memory and emotions entwine, each time she recalls the disturbing incidence, she again feels the original strength of anguish. She can recall a wounding occurrence that happened twenty years ago and experience the same degree of hurt as the day the episode occurred. The fears that she originally associated with the event remain alive and active inside her mind. They cause her to expect similar problems during any future dealings with her offender. This mental record creates a biological handicap she must overcome before she can pardon her offender.

Remembering an emotionally charged scene enlists the left side of a woman's amygdala, but a man primarily employs the right side. Scans of men's brains reveal that they record only a general overview of emotional scenes. Conversely, women register every small, minute detail (Canli et al 2002). Because men store unemotional, sketchy memory of disturbing episodes, they more easily release such memories. Rarely do men waste time dwelling on unpleasant events, and after dismissing the situation, they often question why women cannot also forget what happened, forgive, and let it go. He fails to recognize that it's how God created her. Several weeks after an argument, a husband may not remember the occurrence while his wife lingers in agony.

Judy became embittered when John forgot the topic that triggered their disagreements. She interpreted his forgetting as proof he does not care about her feelings. But he thought about the matter only when she referred to it because the issue didn't bother him as deeply as it had her. Judy could not comprehend John - or any man - forgetting something she considered so significant.

Understanding such differences in gender memory helped John realize why Judy frequently reacted so strongly. It also showed Judy why she required a firm commitment to manage her emotions when upset and wanting to discuss a concern. To keep her promise to change, Judy had to stop replaying messages of how hurt she felt insider her thoughts.

Stopping Rumination

When a woman regurgitates a story of betrayal, eventually, she feels distressed more by her repeated negative thoughts than by what her offender did. Unfortunately, she cannot forgive until she commits to stopping private repetitive thoughts.

Repeating negative thoughts appears to begin at an early age for girls. I have counseling some as young as sixteen who admitted continually dwelling on the ways others hurt her since age six or seven.

Judy's commitment to stop negative thinking required that she agree never to phone her sister or best friend in hope of receiving sympathy. Their support trapped her in a cycle of increased pain until her angry thoughts ultimately hurt her more than anything John did. She needed support to stop such thoughts, not help keeping them alive.

Still, regardless of how bad Judy felt, there remained a choking knot in her heart that insisted she needed to forgive. God put this desire in her to ensure peaceful relationships, and to ensure she knew the Lord expected more from her.

Prayer remains the answer. I know from my own experience and from hours of counseling others that no matter our concern, prayer always works. Saying, "Lord, I am again thinking about this. Please help me stop," reaps immediate success. Calling on God rushes His heavenly response to earth and fills our minds with distracting, positive thoughts. With God's help, we forgive concerns that alone seem impossible. Other techniques that support success include reframing the situation (a later chapter), and some women find writing the details of the situation and then burning the paper works, especially when this includes prayer.

We do not need an apology to forgive – although, in many situations it helps. That's because forgiveness occurs inside our thoughts, and it's what eliminates regurgitating thoughts. We know we have forgiven when we stop dwelling on hurtful situations, end our wallowing in anger, and release all desire for revenge. We may still ache, but we no longer wish for another to do the same. It is not our place to decide if our offenders deserve forgiveness. We only question their merit, if we want an excuse for continued anger.

Jesus told the apostles to forgive a brother (or sister) who repents, no matter how many times the brother sins and asks to be forgiven. The apostles' responded by asking Jesus to increase their faith. Apparently, they knew that to forgive the same person repetitively required more faith than they had, but because the offender was a brother they knew they needed to do as asked. Jesus answered by describing how applying one's faith grows similar to how a planted seed develops. However, to forgive is not for boasting or leaving the brother indebted. Rather, when they forgive they have only behaved as the Lord expects (Luke 17:3-11).

However, Jesus does call us to act smart. He would not expect us to forgive an evil person who raped our child and then leave the helpless child alone with the rapist. He expects us to safeguard ourselves and family from such people. Forgiveness occurs in our hearts and does not imply immediate trust without documented changes in the person's behaviors that align perfectly with their words of regret. Words alone prove insufficient when safety is involved. Read how Joseph tested his brothers multiple times before trusting them (Genesis 42-44). Forgiveness can occur without the offender ever being trustworthy.

However, when it's our ego that's wounded, God requires us to turn the other cheek. Being called rude names, slapped, spit on, or forced to carry more than our share of a load is not life-threatening. Such situations only injure our pride, and most conflicts result because we feel disrespected. Instead of counter-attacking, we need to ask God to repair our egos and open our hearts. We forgive esteem offenses because they prove trivial when compared to our neglect and deliberate disobedience of our Lord, and still He forgives us. We forgive because we do not want to place our prideful feelings above being right with the Lord.

Offering Pardon

Forgiveness is the rare attribute that demonstrates genuine love because it requires sacrificing our human desire to hurt back. We pardon another by setting aside our wounded pride, stopping the self-pity, and altering our hearts and thoughts. Only then do we focus on exoneration. Forgiveness ensures that God's blessings flow for both the forgiven and the forgiver (1 Peter 3:9) because offering pardon is a virtue demonstrating Christ-likeness.

Research finds exchanging rumination of a bad experience with a wider view creates a desire within us to be receptive to forgiving an offender. Researchers, Witvliet, Knoll, Hinman, and DeYoung (2010), offer two ways for reappraising hurtful situations. One requires compassion by acknowledging the offender's humanity and interpreting the wrongdoing as evidence that the offender needs a positive transformation. The second requires self-examination of what you learned about yourself.

Compassion does not demand you forget, or ignore what happened, or deny how painful the experience was. Neither do you absolve the offender of the offense, nor deny your right to be angry. The person inflicted damage, and you have reason to feel upset. But compassion recognizes the offending person's faults and humanness. You acknowledge the person's blemished development, and how it's likely that your offender does not like his flaws, any more than you like your own imperfections. You pity the offender for how he deals with life. When you assess your offender using compassion, your heart opens to forgive. Once you forgive, you feel better about the offender and yourself. Afterwards, you can even pray for the person. Then it's up to the offender to act trustworthy, but inside your heart he's forgiven.

You can then address your own behavior and how you wish you handled the matter differently. You grow by recognizing how you tend to respond to painful situations, how you plan to respond differently in future encounters, and how you can now better empathize with others who experience similar hurts. The researchers discovered that recognizing how you benefited from a bad experience prompts personal happiness and softens the parasympathetic nervous system's negative effects on your heart. Forgiveness frees you of negative thoughts, and your offender may never know or care.

Still, grieving processes your pain in a normal, healthy way. Often, the length of recovery time is proportional to the depth of your pain. Instead of wishing the event had never happened, you heal by accepting what occurred, admitting the wrong, absorbing the pain, and allowing emotional recovery before forgiving.

When I saw John and Judy again they had wallowed in regret long enough. It was time to forgive, forget, and trust.

CHAPTER ELEVEN

FORGIVE – FORGET - TRUST

"Our argument is all I thought about all week. I found myself slamming cabinet doors because I was still upset. I want to stop clinging to hurt and anger. I need to learn how. I am tired of feeling ashamed, and I need to believe that John's really forgiven me." Judy sounded sincere.

John admitted, "I am ashamed and embarrassed to have anyone know how mean I can be. We have to stop acting like this. Seems we have become worse since I lost my job, but my job loss is not a valid reason to behave like I do."

Fortunately, Judy's and John's faith reconciled their human desire to withhold forgiveness. Both admitted their spiritual weaknesses, and both yearned for the comfort of being close again.

.Listening to their recorded argument, Judy and John admitted what they learned about their own behaviors and neither liked what they heard. Their harsh words and John's chilling withdrawal demanded a formal granting of forgiveness. Their shamed consciences elicited a need to confess, repent, and change. Their admission of wrongdoing proved a significant developmental step because blaming another never eases guilt or makes one feel better.

In God's eyes, we do not exist as victims. We live as condemned sinners for what we think, say, and do, and a pierced conscience forces us to accept the truth about ourselves. Such honesty reveals the necessity of Christ's sacrifice to cover our sinful condition. Without Him, we would all be lost. Seeing ourselves as God sees us has us seeking forgiveness, and then, knowing that afterwards, we live acceptable in His sight.

John and Judy wanted to change and live according to Scripture. Born of God, they could not live in hardened rebellion and feel okay. They hated their sinful arguments and felt good about their desire to change.

Self-evaluations

Judy and John discussed their own emotions and behaviors. They identified the top flaws they displayed during their argument and committed to improving. Admitting their own flaws and failings provided an honest mirror of their character. Such admission heightened their desire to change and become a better person. Still, rooting sin from their thoughts, words, and behaviors remains a life-long struggle that requires continual attention.

John's tearful openness in admitting his weaknesses and contempt for his use of mean, abusive words satisfied Judy's craving for deep, tender intimacy. "I hate myself when I talk mean to you. I love you very much, and yet, I often talk to you in ways that make you question this. I hate this trait in me. You deserve much more than you get from me. I know you have times when you need to talk, and I'm unavailable. I want to change that. I want to control my feelings and stop leaving you when you need me. It's hard, very hard, but know that it's what I want to learn to do. No matter what you need from me, I want to be there for you. Honestly, I do. I want us both to know that the other stands beside them no matter the problem. I want you to feel you are more important to me than anything or anyone else in this world. Please, forgive me." John demonstrated a willingness to be emotionally vulnerable and it melted Judy's hurt and anger. She leaped from her chair and wrapped John in her arms, as she cried and pleaded for him to forgive her too.

John's honesty allowed Judy to reply with compassion, rather than rage. His commitment and motivation to change proved how deeply he loves her. Judy's warm responsive hugs and tears showed John how much she appreciated his openness. Her commitment to change assured him how deeply she valued their marriage. They appreciated each other's commitment for remaining together and making their relationship better. Asking God's forgiveness proved their sincerity.

We realize the significance of God's grace when we admit how sinfully we behave. We receive grace not because we are good, or because we deserve forgiveness, but because God loves us, wretched as we are. Thankfully, Jesus died for the ungodly (Romans 5:6).

Judy and John admitted they wanted to put to death the deeds of the body and live for Christ (Romans 8:12-13). They agreed that being right with God remained more important than having one's way or feeling valued by each other. They sounded determined to put the Lord first.

John and Judy identified ways they knew the other wished they had behaved differently. Answering, "If your spouse could relive the episode, what do you think he/she would now say or do differently?" reassured them that they believed the other wanted to act respectfully.

They shared one trait they appreciate about the way the other responds while upset and asked permission to keep one behavior that often annoyed the other. John liked how Judy remains receptive to reconnecting and wanted to keep having some alone time. "I promise to quit leaving the house when I am upset, but I do need some quiet time alone when we disagree. I need to think through how I want to behave and what I can do to help resolve our differences. I can't do it if we are in the same room because one of us wants to say more. I need quiet time to think. I need you to give me space for having time alone. I know this bothers you but I really need it."

Judy appreciated how John tended to take the initiative for making-up, and she told John, "When I cry, it is because I am genuinely hurting. I can't stand us being estranged. I need to feel close to you every minute of every day. That sounds unrealistic, but it's what I want and what I need. So, when I cry it's because I need to feel closer to you than I currently am. Crying is not to control or manipulate you. I promise. I need you to understand and make it okay for me to cry."

John used quiet time alone and Judy cried as a way of protecting, nurturing, and calming themselves. Such actions carried no intent to create frustration or sadness. They don't fully understand the other's needs, but they can accept that it helped them to calm and reduced a desire for fight or flight.

Instead of trying to make each other conform, Judy and John agreed to give up unenforceable rules about how the other should behave and committed to discussing daily discomforts when they happen. No one is strong enough to live up to another's expectations consistently as they admitted when confessing how they frequently failed to live by God's.

Forgiving John's Company and Manager

In addition, they discussed their feelings about John's prior company and the supervisor who terminated John. They needed to mourn the loss of their wishful dreams and goals and forgive the manager. Instead of anger and resentment, they felt grief and sadness and displaced their disappointment on each other. Fighting distracted them from their true emotions. They mourned the loss of plans and hopes they now realized would never materialize. John admitted, "I always saw myself retiring from this company. It's a great place to work, and I was promoted twice. I liked what I did and the people. Now I worry about having money today, not just in retirement." John missed his job terribly.

Judy bemoaned the fact that, "I like living near my parents. They are elderly and will soon need help. Plus, it is nice to have them take the kids for a couple of weeks in the summer and let us share time alone. If we ever had an emergency, I know they would be available to care for the children and that means a lot.

By sympathizing with the boss' vulnerable role of being the bearer of tragic news, they no longer needed to displace their grief and disappointment onto each other. It freed them to create new plans and new dreams.

Impact on Kids

Lastly, they discussed the impact their hostile arguments made on their children. Judy admitted that her commitment to change provided a gift for the children, even more than for herself or John. "I feel terrible about what I am teaching my children. They deserve more than I am giving them. I am going to change so they can know how to have a happy marriage themselves. I am going home today and ask them to forgive me. I am going to pray daily with them for all of us to speak kindly to each other. It will become a part of our breakfast prayer."

In addition, Judy suggested that she would agree with whatever rule John made about the kids chores. She admitted being too lenient with things they could responsibly handle. Making the children do things they didn't want to do left her feeling like the 'bad guy' of the family, and she avoided her parental responsibility by making John handle all discipline.

John suggested he would make a list of tasks the kids could do and let Judy approve it before showing it to the kids. They agreed to explain the chores to the kids together and insist that they both expected the tasks completed. If she disagreed with John about discipline, Judy promised to tell him privately – never again in hearing of the children.

In exchange, John promised he would stop suggesting they borrow money from his parents. He agreed to sell their new car or borrow on their house mortgage from the bank if necessary.

Curtailing Judy's Angry Outbursts

Before leaving, Judy admitted she needed help in curing her use of angry words when she approached John to talk about disturbing concerns. Had her outbursts not occasionally reaped what she wanted, she would have ended her use of them long ago. John reinforced Judy's use of rude words by stopping what he was doing and meeting her demands just often enough for her to continue. Judy's use of sharp words needed to fail consistently. She acknowledged the importance of making the change and asked for John's assistance.

John agreed not to respond if Judy opened a dialogue using a rude method. He could look away or begin humming, but he should avoid looking in Judy's direction, never respond, and not leave. If Judy began a conversation using a tone John found annoying but not overtly hostile, he agreed to answer by whispering, so she had to strain to hear what he said. She agreed that John's whispering would signal her to speak softer.

Judy agreed that if she again used either approach, she would punish herself just like one of the kids and go to bed early without dinner or TV time. Even if she had plans, she would cancel them. Self-punishment would come first. She promised to lie in bed praying and asking God to help her realize what she should have said differently. The following morning she would ask John's forgiveness and repeat the same request but in a polite way.

If Judy opened her dialogue using kind words, John offered to put his arms around her and ask, "What can I do to help?" Judy assured him that a hug would help her remember to speak kindly. He offered to hug her consistently each time she began talking with gentle words. After continually hugging her for a few weeks, John needed to shift to hugging her occasionally. Rewarding another using a varied schedule of reinforcement ensures the desired change becomes permanent. John's hugging Judy consistently for six or seven weeks and then only occasionally should ensure that Judy remembered to think about how she wanted to speak.

Whispering and hugging offered John some control over Judy's unkind ways of initiating discussions. He provided the strength to help Judy overcome a weakness that hurt their marriage.

Judy and John needed to deal swiftly and quickly with sin. Stopping sinful thoughts the moment they germinate inhibits them from becoming words or actions. Sin must be deprived of its strength and rooted out before anger swells. They must do it themselves. No one can do it for them. The best way to break any bad habit is to replace it with a healthier one, like prayer that asks God to change their thoughts when thinking negatively.

They agreed if either spoke using rude words in their children's presence they would stop immediately and pray aloud, asking God and their children to forgive them. Judy and John proved that blessings can exist in dire circumstances, and finally, they prepared to receive them.

God's challenge for many couples is learning to respond in what may seem an unnatural way. Couples can reappraise their thoughts about negative situations and empathize with the partner's faults and weaknesses while still hating what the spouse did. By stopping their use of angry words, they replace sinful habits with moral ones (1 Corinthians 6:18) and grow in the Lord by meditating daily on His Word (Psalm 1:2; 119:105). When the Word begins to control their hearts and thoughts, it confronts and attacks the sin in their lives.

Judy's and John's openness reduced their months of bitterness. They committed to discussing issues without becoming aggressively antagonistic. Still, conflict is inevitable and agreeing to ask God's forgiveness in the presence of their children served as a powerful deterrent to relapsing.

Ask: What's Right for Our relationship?

Daily, we face the choice of choosing to love. Every situation becomes a test of putting one value before another. Growth comes by asking with every frustrating event, "In this situation, what's the right thing for me to do for our relationship?" Asking shifts the focus away from self and directs it to the need of the relationship as a unit. Just asking the question reduces selfishness. A good marriage develops when the highest priority of a husband and wife is doing what's right for their relationship with the Lord and then with each other, rather than for self. From Genesis through Revelation we are instructed to do what's right, and making the question personal with the words "right thing **for me to do**" forces us to personally apply the command to daily situations.

Matthew (15:40) tells us when we do good for another, we do good for the Lord. God takes how we treat each other extremely personal. That alone remains reason enough to keep our mates happy.

How We Disagree Matters

Research shows that what we argue about is not what is important. Neither is the frequency we disagree. What matters is how we argue. We must learn to disagree politely. Otherwise, we create a history of continual turmoil. All couples disagree, and research proves that couples who view their marital history in negative ways increase their likelihood of divorcing (Gottman 1999). We need to dwell on current, positive times because thinking about our good times overshadows bad experiences.

Once Judy and John believed they would receive forgiveness rather than abandonment, their home became calmer. Private, personal fears diminished greatly. However, since stress remains a normal part of life, they still needed to learn ways for short-circuiting their sympathetic nervous system when feeling anxious. Learning to control their feelings ensures they avoid becoming upset and choosing fight or flight.

Judy asked if she could come alone for the next session. She wanted some girl-talk about how to feel comfortable when John became upset and wanted time by himself. John's withdrawal triggered high anxiety for Judy, and she wanted to keep her promise to give him quiet time without her interference.

CHAPTER TWELVE

GIVE HIM A TIME-OUT

Judy asked how she could feel comfortable when she and John argued and he wanted time by himself. I reminded her of what he said when he joined her in counseling. "Judy makes every disagreement into a full-blown theatrical production. Even minor ones. She magnifies everything I say that isn't what she wants to hear. I have to get away from her to calm." Like most husbands, John wanted quick solutions for resolving heated disagreements. He hated discord.

I explained to Judy that most husbands hate an intense dispute. A man resents his wife continuing to talk. Her complaining sounds mean, and he wants to escape. Once upset, talking is the last thing he thinks about doing. Instead, he wants quiet time alone and out of hearing distance. It's as if a man's mind goes immediately blank. He can't talk until he calms and comes up with options, while a woman instantly wants to talk because she thinks concerns through by talking them through.

A couple's sympathetic system charges when a disagreement turns heated. Aroused, their hormones prepare them for fight or flight. Men choose flight in an attempt to reduce their physiological arousal because most men find hyper-arousal unbearable. They cannot think. Their mind goes numb. To survive, they jump in the car and go for a drive, jog around the block, or slip outside and work in the yard. While a man rarely tells himself that his wife doesn't love him, he thinks she doesn't like or respect him. At that moment, he doesn't like her so much either. However once he calms, he wants to feel close again. At the peak of high emotion, he may not like her so much, but he knows he loves her and wants their relationship to work. He pulls away because it allows him time to calm so he can return and talk better later. While away in his isolated, mental man cave, he thinks about their differences. A man yearns for closeness as much as a woman does, but while loaded with strong emotional, he remains unable to process ideas for increasing their relationship security by immediately talking.

A man amid a heated disagreement feels similar to how you feel when you are having a terrible, awful, low-down, no good day and then your toddler throws spinach at you, dumps some atop his head, and the rest on the floor. Then has a screaming melt-down when you say, "No, don't throw food." You know you love and cherish the child, but right then you could give him away. You wish grandmother would unexpectedly stop by, help clean the mess, and take him to park for an hour, maybe a week. At that moment, the child's behavior feels too personal. You wish you could get away from the child, avoid the mess, and just have some time for yourself. Why? So you can return more loving as you care for your child. Your husband feels similarly during a heated argument..

A husband needs quiet time alone to cool and decide how to handle differences without his wife's interruptions. He seeks time and space to think. The deeper his hurt, the longer it takes him to calm. Some disagreements cause such anguish, he needs hours to calm; others he resolves quickly.

Unlike his wife, a man doesn't telephone a friend and admit to arguing, unless he's at the divorce stage. He doesn't seek outside support because he doesn't want others to know. He wants time alone to process a way for resolving the matter. That requires him to compartmentalize the disagreement into its own separate mental box and stop dwelling on it. Once he boxes his feelings, his parasympathetic system calms. He exits his mental man cave and returns with hope of talking in a way that creates reconciliation.

Some husbands who take flight believe their wives also values time alone. These men think leaving is a way of protecting her from his anger. Others become so upset that they use it as another way of punishing her. They know she's hurting, and at that moment, they don't care. Regardless of the reason, the distance and time apart make the situation unbearable for her.

She interprets his actions as telling her that he doesn't care about her or their relationship. That he no longer loves her. However, if he did stay and attempt to discuss the issue further, many women would escalate their bitter words, and a full-blown skirmish would ensue.

When a husband walks out during an argument, his wife tends to panic. She feels torturous, something she can't bear. She does not sense estrangement; she suffers with strong feelings of desertion and abandonment. The intense activation of her sympathetic system makes her emotions unbearable, and she is terrified feeling so disconnected. Because women process their feeling by talking about the issue, she can't understand his not wanting to discuss the matter.

Only a man doesn't think things through by talking about them. He doesn't have the multiple connections between the left and right hemispheres of his brain as she does. He can't talk about feelings and thoughts at the same time. While she feels better when she discusses negative feelings, he feels worse. He's an internal processer who prefers thinking about one issue at a time - alone. Lacking all the mental wiring to connect feelings, thoughts and words for talking, he goes inside and resolves his options before discussing possibilities.

Few wives understand a husband's desire to withdraw because she wants to pull closer. For her, they are already too divided. The farther her husband pulls away physically, the deeper she hungers for emotional closeness. She yearns for him to come put his arms around her.

However, a hug is the last thing an upset husband wants. His wife's quarrelsome words repulse him, and he can't imagine her wanting a hug while so emotional. Besides, he can't comfort her. His wounded heart aches. At that moment, he faces hostile warfare. She is the enemy, and no man hugs his enemy. He feels vulnerable, confused, and often ashamed because he didn't handle the issue differently. With so many feelings swirling in his head, he can't think, and he can't talk until he can think.

Because a wife fears her husband might not return, or at least not for hours, she may attempt to prevent his leaving. She fails to realize that any attempt to stop his escape increases his anger and subjugates his attempts at self-control. Her attempt to stop his escape lengthens the time it takes for him to calm. She doesn't realize this because she focuses exclusively on alleviating her own pain.

Self-management Practice for Judy

How men and women experience different needs while upset proved a valuable lesson for Judy. She failed to realize that she and John were giving to each other what they wanted for themselves. Both believed they were doing what would improve their relationship and that the other betrayed their marriage.

Judy admitted, "So you are telling me that I behave in ways that make things worse for John. I want to feel close so badly that I panic when he leaves me. I need him, and he walks away. I don't know how many times I have stood in the doorway trying to block it so he can't exit. If he does get past me, I follow him to the garage and grab the car door so he can't close it. I hold tight, as if my life depends on it because, for me, at the moment it does. I am losing the one person who means the most to me. Now you are telling me that my actions are the worst thing I could do to have John desire closeness."

Judy confirmed that when the need God placed in a woman to bond with her man faces direct assault, she thinks only about her desire to remain physically close. Judy thought if they stayed near each other, they could talk and work through the dividing issue. She repeatedly told herself that they could not resolve issues while apart. Judy could not comprehend John's need for time alone because she thought only about how she felt. But John wasn't rejecting Judy. Rather, he rejected resolving the issue her way. God didn't wire him to resolve things by talking like a woman does.

Judy needed reassurance John's leaving did not imply he no longer loved her or that he intended to leave permanently. Rather, his walking out meant he wanted to reduce his anger and feel better so he could return and talk. Unfortunately, the more Judy attempted to restrain John, the stronger his urge to leave, and the longer he stayed away.

This new information proved a real eye-opener for Judy. She committed to trusting the accuracy of such counsel and agreed to give John time alone. She promised to abstain from any behavior that would hinder John's leaving. After all, if John wanted quiet time to decide how to resolve their estrangement so they could reconnect and talk, why would she block that?

Judy needed to learn how to better control her emotions when John left. I suggested that Judy leave also and go do something for herself that she would enjoy. The distraction would calm and soothe her raw emotions.

"I don't know what I would like. My days are filled with the kids' activities and working around John's schedule. I rarely do anything just for myself."

Judy promised to make a list of five things she would enjoy doing without John or the children. If a disagreement escalated, she agreed to do at least one thing on her list. I suggested she not return for counseling for a few weeks and see how they handled differences. If they experienced another strong disagreement, she could schedule another appointment. It was four weeks before I saw them again.

Realizing When Erred

Judy prepared a cake for her dad's surprise birthday party. All the family was attending and she offered to bring the cake. While the cake baked, her son opened the oven door to peek inside, and when he let the door slam shut, the cake fell. Judy bit her tongue and told her son it would still taste the same, but she felt like crying. Later, when John came in and opened the oven door to see what smelled so good, she exploded. She wasn't upset with John. The cake had already fallen. She was annoyed with her son, and embarrassed at the thought of taking an ugly cake to her dad's party, and sad that she couldn't afford to buy him a prettier one. John reaped her frustration. She yelled at him with a rude, cutting remark, and John immediately turned to walk to the car.

Realizing her error, Judy knew John's leaving was her fault. She explained, "This time, I did nothing and said nothing to stop him. Instead, I sat down and grabbed a Bible. But I admit that I just stared at the open pages. I was too upset with myself to read. So, I prayed, asking God to forgive me and for John to calm quickly. But, you will be proud of me that I didn't try to stop his leaving."

Judy proved that when a person's parasympathetic becomes highly aroused, we still have choices about how we behave. We do not have to allow our emotions to control our behavior. We do not have to cave to the desire to fight or flee. Self-protection is rarely necessary, regardless of how strongly we feel it is.

John confessed, "I pretended to ignore Judy's silence, but I was well aware of it. As usual, I rushed to the car and sat down. Then I remembered my promise not to leave when upset. Judy kept her promise to understand my need for quiet time, and I knew I also needed to keep my word. So, I came back inside and went to the bedroom. I pouted, felt sorry for myself, and prayed. Then I thought about ways to handle our issue. Once I resolved this inside my thoughts I asked Judy to talk. I had to know how to handle the matter before I could talk with her. It's like she immediately knew but I didn't. When I asked her to talk, I think she was shocked."

John did not leave. When Judy hushed her fight- attack words and acted as if she didn't care that he left, John discontinued his flight - leave response. He made a different choice. He, too, over-rode his fight-flight arousal. He made a mental decision to keep his word, rather than allowing his feelings to control his conduct.

This was the first time John asked to discuss a disagreement so soon after an argument. When Judy allowed John peaceful, uninterrupted time, he returned prepared to re-connect and satisfy her desire to communicate. When Judy let John have a time-out at home without her continuing to talk, he resolved the issue inside his thoughts and sought to reestablish closeness. A husband cannot stand feelings of alienation any more than a wife.

Reconnect Emotionally

A temporary time-out allows temper's coded distress signals of a raised voice, a red face, an increased heart beat, or the use of stinging words to calm. Such reactions signal that a couple is polarized. They can set a time to come together again and finish the discussion but only after emotions calm. Taking a break to pray and think about ways for resolving the matter ensures that neither partner internalizes enough pressure for fighting or fleeing. They need to remind themselves that it is okay to have desires, and it is okay for the spouse to have different ones.

Prayer makes the self-protection of fight-flight unnecessary because God requires that we examine our own hearts, not another's. After praying, God ensures that both spouses possess a desire for bonding. This allows us to begin our discussion in a more positive mood, and we solve more issues when neither responds with anger.

When a husband and wife become angry, and she gives him uninterrupted time alone, he calms and hopes to reestablish closeness. If he takes the initiative for reconciling, a wife needs to be amicable because a man remains sensitive to signals of rejection. A wife should swallow her pride and act receptive (Luke 17:4), because if she refuses his offer, he may be less willing to connect later. The longer a detachment continues the more difficult it becomes to reestablish closeness because egos expand and block resolution.

If upon his return, the husband seems hesitant to make up, she needs to park her ego and step forward. Reestablishing closeness is the goal, not who moves first.

Giving a man a time out without her talking proved a worthwhile lesson for Judy. Because she felt successful, she asked for other ways for them to acquire a deeper emotional closeness. For her that meant having John share how he felt about things. Judy no longer sought help for leaving John; she now asked for assistance in drawing him closer.

CHAPTER THIRTEEN

TEACH HIM FEELING TALK

"I often feel overwhelmed with all my family expects me to do. The kid's activities never end, and most days John keeps his head buried in the computer with his job search. We rarely talk, not real talk. No intimate talk. We argue less, but that isn't enough. I crave attention, and adult conversation. With us having no money, we never do anything fun anymore. What if he goes months and months without a job?" Judy could not hide her frustration.

I agreed with her. Judy did need more, but not necessarily more of what she wanted and not in ways she envisioned. Too often, the ways she attempted to have John understand her needs failed to solicit cooperation. Judy needed to realize the source of conflict before she could alter her pattern. She needed to understand that women have acted like she often does since the beginning of time. Understanding why, she could change her approach.

Conflict Began in the Garden

Before they sinned, Adam and Eve experienced oneness as together they ruled the earth. However, after eating the forbidden fruit, their immediate reaction was to disconnect and hide. Psychologically, their relationship with God and each other changed dramatically. Shame and desire to avoid exposure replaced vulnerability and intimacy. Now Adam and Eve experienced disagreements, and each claimed the other was to blame.

God punished Eve for her sinful choice. She would struggle forever with desire for Adam to satisfy her longings. "Your desire will be for your husband, and he will rule over you" (Genesis 3:16). Eve's thoughts centered on her relationship with Adam. Adam's focus became the painful toil of making a living (Genesis 3:17-20). God required Adam to work for his livelihood and to sacrifice the best of his labor. Adam didn't have to be perfect, but his sacrifice needed to please the Lord. Life changed for man and for woman. They no longer bonded in close intimate ways. Woman pursued love from her man while the man worked and sought respect for his sacrifices.

Eve's Punishment Governs

Wives, like Judy, long for a deeper emotional closeness with their husbands. Their desire mirrors the relationship God yearns to have with us, but instead of turning to the Lord, many women expect their husbands to fill their emotional hunger exclusively. Then when he fails, their longing becomes the cause of marital discord. They react like Eve, deciding what they will and will not tolerate and what they will do about it, rather than designing their lives by God's plan.

". . . and he will rule over you" (Genesis 3:16) is God's stern punishment for Eve's sinful choice. Relationships became a source of problems and conflict, rather than ongoing joy as God intended originally. The consequence was that wives crave closeness with their husbands, and husbands decide the degree of closeness. He rules over her.

Whoever controls what you want holds the power in your relationship. When another has something you desire, the person can choose when, how often, and how much you receive. The person rules the relationship because your desire crowns him with authority.

God's discipline for woman proved a penalty for the wife and a testing for her husband. To lessen the severity on women, God, in His loving kindness, commands a husband to love his wife as he loves his own body (Ephesians 5:28). A husband's test is to learn to love his wife in ways she values. Loving his wife as his own body ensures a husband does not mistreat her or ignore her desires but strives to satisfy her needs.

Because a man's needs differ, most men think they contribute to their marriages as much as their wives. Or, almost as much. For him, being home together means that he is working on their relationship.

The problem lies in how each views a home. A man views his home as a place of comfort and quiet, a place he can escape the day's demands. Home for him represents a place of solitude where he shuts out the rest of the world.

A woman considers home a place she can say what she really feels and have her feelings accepted. She yearns for a deep connection. She does not measure her husband's support by how much time he spends at home, as much as by the degree of personal information they share. If her void of intimate talk continues too long, she questions her value for their marriage.

He Equates Withholding with Support

Some men view their withholding information about their daily activities from their wives as a demonstration of caring. He thinks it's a way to protect her from concerns he finds frustrating. He reasons, "Why should I discuss negative situations and cause her to feel bad too?" But if he shares only what he would tell a neighbor, he fails to supply sufficient information to satisfy her.

The more negative a man's day at work, the less desire he holds for discussing that day's events at home (Schulz et al 2004). But a wife suffers a high degree of loneliness when she believes there is not enough sharing of daily details. The husband has no idea the degree of information his wife requires because companionship for him means time together, not interacting while together. He views his withholding such negativity as a form of protection, while she calls it rejection.

Few wives can comprehend how a man would consider that withholding anything from them proves caring. However, they can trust that it is their husband's intent, and he believes he acts supportive.

Emotional love for a wife includes talking about private, personal feelings. But some days she feels as if she's still trying to communicate with a teenager who, when asked did you have a good day replies, "Nope," and walks out the door. She not only wants to hear every detail of her husband's day, she wants to know how he feels about each incident. Men rarely understand the depth of intimacy a woman desires.

The problem is that a man never thinks about including how he feels about anything. A man who details his day with brief, factual words considers it a thorough explanation. Highlighting the main events, a man thinks he has shared completely.

He Freezes with Emotional Pressure

Two sentences husbands hate hearing are: "We need to talk," and "How did you feel?" A man does not automatically know how he feels about anything. A woman instantly knows how she feels, but a man doesn't. He must pause and process his thoughts. Her annoyance numbs his thinking because he knows from her body language how upset she is. He forgets trying to decide how he feels and tries to determine how he can avoid upsetting her.

When a woman talks over or interrupts a man, it takes him twice as long to gather his thoughts. Typically, he goes silent, but if he does talk, often he attempts to shift the subject. Her interruption shifts his thinking away from the original topic. The wife needs to pause, slow down, and gather her thoughts about what words to use.

Learn by Observing

Watching how your husband communicates with another man can show you how to increase your man's desire to talk. You will note how his listener never responds critically and never offers suggestions unless asked. The listener listens quietly, smiles, and occasionally nods his head. Once your husband pauses, the listener asks questions related to the subject. Why does your husband continue talking? The listener's behaviors show that your husband's story is worth hearing, and men strive to act respectfully to each other when they speak.

Try using the same method when your husband mentions a sporting event or new car model. Be sensitive to his areas of interest and what they mean to him. If you want to hear about personal topics, show interest in the impersonal subjects he likes to discuss. If you want him acknowledging your interests, then show respect for his.

Keep your body language like another man's: Smile, nod, and shake your head in agreement. Speak only after he pauses. Offer questions, not suggestions. Above all, stay on topic – his topic. Do not interject all the connected issues you think of, regardless of how significant you consider the related topics. Your brain's connected wires will likely link his comments to multiple side issues, but remember, he communicates from a single box. If you bring up a related issue that changes the subject, he will likely shut down and regret sharing with you. He chose the topic, so let him control the subject, and stay with him. Follow his lead.

Feeling talk comes natural for few men. Someone must show them how to express private emotional thoughts. Who better than his wife?

Teach with Questions

A wife teaches her husband intimate relating by demonstrating its use, not with lectures or reprimands. If she practices what she wants from him, then her husband learns by noting how he feels after each discussion. If he finds he likes talking with her, he will want to communicate the same way but usually to a lesser degree.

For example, when your husband discloses a tidbit of information instead of responding with, "You could have - should have - done it this way," show interest by nodding your head in agreement. To a man, could of - should of sounds disrespectful, like you are calling him stupid or a failure for what he did. Interjecting the possibility of a different approach sets up competition. He hears you implying, "I am wiser than you, and if you had done things my way, your results would be better." You want him sharing, not competing. A woman needs to hit her pause button and listen, not make suggestions

Instead, replace your stream of ideas with thoughtful questions. Asking questions about his topic helps him remember more details for sharing. The more questions you ask, the longer your husband will talk because it shows you are interested. Questions show you care about his interest and indicate you are eager to understand why the subject appeals to him.

To learn how he feels about an issue and the ways he may have struggled, you can ask, "How did you handle that? It must have been challenging." Saying, "Was that a difficult decision for you?" and "How do you think your decision will impact others?" reveal his degree of comfort with an outcome. When you ask, "What do you think your boss thought about you doing it this way?" your question elicits his perception of the boss' idea and his reaction to the manager. Saying, "Do you know how proud I am of your decision?" ensures that he knows how you like hearing his ideas.

Ask questions to solicit the emotional information you want from him. He will respond if you appear eager to hear more. You will find that your man can talk as long and as deeply as you can if you provide him the correct verbal and non-verbal feedback. Using questions prove you care about what interests him and you want to understand his ideas. The right questions have your husband sharing intimate details he would never reveal to a neighbor.

Help Him Understand Your Feelings

More often, what women desire is for their husbands to listen and understand how they feel about issues or specific people. That's because a woman wants her man to validate her feelings when she's upset, regardless of why she's distressed. His using words that show he understands and cares that she's hurting remains more valued by her than knowing how he feels about any topic.

Again, help him understand how you care about a topic by asking questions. While communicating your story, interject questions to ensure your husband understands. For example, say, "What do you think about what I did?" "Can you understand why it makes me feel so good?" "Can you comprehend why it seems critical to me?" "How could I have reacted differently?" "Can you imagine what I really wanted to say to her?" "Do you know why I feel so rotten?" "Can you understand why the idea of doing it scares me?" "Can you see why I fought fight back tears?" "What would you have done in my place?" Do not let your man remain unresponsive. Instead, challenge him with questions. Questions let him realize what is relevant to you and to grasp your emotional connection to the situation. Ask, and his answers will produce the intimate closeness you seek.

Occasionally pause to hug him and say, "Your listening helps me focus my thoughts. You are helpful that way." Thanking him ensures he knows you relish his comments and appreciate his trying to understand. If you want more feeling talk, ask questions to guarantee you receive it.

Women need to accept that most men listen more with their intellect than their emotions. A man does not grasp the needs his wife is attempting to relate automatically, especially if she makes an indirect request like, "You are never here for me." Another woman understands the meaning, but a man hears it as a complaint, and he has no idea how to improve things. All he knows is he is standing right beside her and came directly home from work. I've had men ask, "What more could she want? I'm standing right there."

The problem reflects both sexes different ways of listening, caring and bonding. Both strive to achieve a loving relationship and go about it in their own unique ways. They do not understand each other's efforts because such differences started at a very young age.

Differences Begin in Childhood

Observe young children. Girls show interest in boys earlier than boys notice girls. In fact, the primary topic girls discuss at a sleep-over is boys. Girls sit on the sideline of a ball field, not to watch the game, but to see the boys present. At the same age, boys focus on activities and winning. They put energy into winning the largest trophy and being the team champion. They focus on competing and disarming their opponents.

Not only do young children concentrate on dissimilar topics, but the distinct ways they communicate begin at an early age.

A girl asks questions that allow her to tell what she thinks, but only after another responds. She shares secrets and uses words like always and never to emphasize the strength of her feelings. When she wants another to do something, she uses the word, "Lets . . . " while a boy barks a command of "You . . . " She pushes for cooperation; he shouts orders to gain control (Tannen 1990).

A boy bonds around activities, not sharing private information. A boy uses sarcasm, put-downs, and cockiness for maintaining status and independence. The boy who receives the put-down rarely takes the comment personally. Afterwards, the boys can enjoy lunch together and act like best pals, but a girl could never eat with someone who made a rude comment to her or about her. Trait differences extend throughout adulthood.

Don't Pout, Ask

Women need to ask for what they want without expressing such emotionality. Sharing feelings helps a woman bond with another woman, but it conflicts with a man's thought processes. He tunes out when there is too much drama because emotions regulate differently in his brain. He doesn't get it. He can't get it. And he can't change so he does. Remember, he didn't design his mental wiring. God did.

Men respond best to direct, rational requests, and they seldom recognize hints. To a man, a hint represents a woman commenting about trivia that he doesn't need to remember. He fails to take her subtle suggestion as something he should do.

Men tend to label women who make indirect comments as manipulative, and she views her approach as being supportive without demanding or controlling. He views his own way of communicating as descriptive and factual. She views his style as too aloof and reserved. Women make indirect requests when they want help with household tasks or the children.

Men speak indirectly when sharing personal information. Both dislike that trait in the other.

Judy's Indirect Approach

Examine Judy's ways for expressing her concerns when John received a job offer in another state. She hated the idea of relocating so far away from family. She read news articles about the company and what she discovered worried her. The articles hinted the company might file bankruptcy. She feared the move might create additional problems.

Judy was so thankful John had a job she didn't want to tell him what she feared or ask him to read the articles. Instead, she frequently commented about how difficult packing is or asked how they would manage their puppy. Occasionally, she questioned if he cared that the kids would lose regular contact with grandparents. Other times, Judy asked non-specific questions about the company, like how John knew the organization was a good place to work. Judy wasn't sure if she feared the company would file bankruptcy or her parents might become ill and need her, so she hid her uneasiness. She risked an expensive move rather than openly expressing her apprehensions and asking questions so John could address her worries. Judy missed an opportunity for helping John weigh all concerns.

Men view money as a way of obtaining status, power, and control, so John's focus on what the new job provided proved very different from Judy's. She evaluated John's job from a woman's need for security and self-sufficiency to ensure she never needed to rely on others.

When stressed and making important decisions, men often overrate aspects that appear rewarding and ignore information predicting possible negative outcomes. For example, when job searching, a man is likely to inflate the value of a pay increase, his title, and vacation time, but underestimate the inconvenience of a long commute, the poor reputation of the person who would be his boss, or the work hours. Stressed, men tend to place rewards near the top of their goals, even to the point they increase risk-taking behaviors, whereas, women take a safer route. (Mather and Lighthall 2012). With Judy's insights, John would not be driven predominately by pecuniary interest and would have weighed her concerns as well.

Many women behave like Judy. Even when their husbands would benefit from feedback about their decisions, they fail to speak directly. They drop hints, ask partially related questions, and avoid speaking frankly, but being respectful and helpful includes her sharing all concerns. Women help their husbands by offering different opinions, and being a husband's helper is a reason God created woman (Genesis 2:18).

Saying What You Don't Want, Fails

Many women complain about what they dislike instead of asking for what they want. A woman says, "You are never here for me anymore," when she could describe, "We have not spent enough time together lately. Will you cuddle with me on the couch tonight and watch a movie? I need to feel close again."

She complains, "You tell the neighbor more about your project than me," but reaps better results by stating what she wants. "It's important to me to know the details first and hear them from you, not through neighborhood gossip. So, will you, please, tell me before anyone else?"

She grumbles, "We never do anything romantic anymore," instead of taking charge, sending the kids to grandmother's, digging a sexy gown from the bottom drawer, reserving a table at a nice restaurant, and booking a hotel room. A woman is capable of ensuring that she gets what she wants when she is willing to step outside her comfort zone.

When you ask indirectly, with words like, "You never . . ." A husband rarely understands what you mean. Your words imply, "What you are doing is not okay. You are failing. You are wrong." And no husband wants to feel such disrespect.

Specific Requests

When a woman expresses what she wants with indirect messages, she leaves her husband presuming what pleases her, guessing wrong much of the time, and trying to determine why she acts disappointed or even angry. He moves into the doghouse without knowing why.

Husbands hate playing a guessing game about what their wives want and like. They relish honesty and sincerity. When a wife speaks straightforwardly about what she wants, her husband can respond to her, rather than speculating what she means. Because no man reads minds, life functions better for both if she describes what she wants in detail. If there is a place you want to eat, tell him. Don't say, "Any place you want," and then become upset when he chooses a restaurant where you would never eat. Do not say, "Any movie you want to see," and later, mention how you wanted to see another. Answering with, "I don't care," comes across as apathy, not genuine interest.

Household Tasks

A primary source of frustration for women is how responsible they feel for the majority of household chores. A woman needs to learn to ask her husband for help using words that describe specifically what she wants him to do. Acting respectful requires asking for help, instead of waiting and hoping he will offer and becoming upset when he doesn't.

However, many women do not want to ask for help at all. They tell themselves that their husbands see all the chores and reasons, "I shouldn't have to ask." She thinks, *"If my husband loved me as I love him, he would know I need help."* Pooh!

That is immature, pink-brain thinking. Either she asks or she suffers self-inflicted, self-pitying misery.

Remember, blue boxes clog a husband's brain and a blue film covers his eyes and ears. He rarely notices your workload. Tell him what you want, and keep the message short. He doesn't need to know what a difficult day you had, or what you must finish before going to bed, or how much you have to do tomorrow. You do not need to justify your request. He lives there too and can help. Do not allow excess talk give him a reason for ignoring you. If he asks, "What's the point you are trying to make?" you have talked too long. A man ignores peripheral details and listens for the central point. Ask quickly and be brief.

However, some men must be asked three or four times before they respond. A couple of things contribute to his slow response. First, men consider that some chores belong to a man, like mowing the lawn, and others to a woman, like dusting. These men rarely think about cutting into her domain unless asked. Second, he may be entrenched in his Empty box. If some past or future activity controls his thoughts, he fails to hear whatever is said. He must first return his attention to the present. She needs to remember that repeating a request to an Empty box beats doing the tasks alone.

Afterward, she should thank him for helping. Respect his willingness to do as requested.

Novel Involvements Improve Marriage

Rather than holding an infantile expectation of finding someone willing to accept responsibility for our desires, we women need to develop interests outside our marriages. We need goals of our own. The more challenging our outside involvement, the fewer demands we make of our husbands. Stay-at-home moms, like Judy, benefit greatly from goals that have them conversing frequently with other women.

Judy agreed to find an outside involvement she would enjoy alone, one that would involve physical activity to help reduce her stress. Solo time could help her realize how she took John's attention for granted. But instead, Judy found an activity to share with John, something he'd said he'd always wanted to do. She registered them to take swimming lessons at their local YMCA. The lessons cost pennies and exercising helped calm their pent-up stress. They even found themselves laughing together again. Then, Judy joined a women's weekly book club through her local library and insisted that once John accepted a new job she planned to learn a foreign language.

Women, like Judy, benefit from accepting responsibility for making their lives meaningful. They demand less from their spouses when they have enjoyable activities of their own. What matters is doing something they like. Once responsible for satisfying their own involvements, they no longer appear clingy or needy, and expect their husbands to make them happy. They bring new interests to the relationship as Judy did by sharing a mini-review of some of the books she read when John asked about it. By filling part of her own emotional hole, Judy stopped pursuing John continuously and felt less lonely when he worked on the computer.

Change Can Make a Spouse Uncomfortable

At first, Judy's small change made John uncomfortable. "I felt abandoned, like she was enjoying not having me around. I guess it's how she felt while I worked on resumes. I worried that she might like being with these other people more than with me. It made me realize how accustomed I was to having her available when I wanted her attention. It proved unpleasant for me for several weeks, especially when I wanted to ask her something and she was buried in a book, or dinner was late because she wanted to finish a chapter. Then I realized how much she enjoyed her activity, and now I am proud of her."

When Judy stopped her continual chase of John for attention, he pursued her by asking for a mini-review of what she read. Judy loved having John pursue her for a change.

Research reveals when a couple undertakes a new involvement, it creates a positive impact in their marriage. Helen Fisher, author of *Why Him? Why Her?* (2009), conducted PET scans of the brains of people who recently fell in love and scans of couples married and still in love after two decades. While sharing exciting activities with their partners, the brains of both groups responded to feelings of reward and satisfaction. The brains of longer married people displayed as much activity as the brains of newly smitten sweethearts excited about bonding a new relationship. Fisher proved that doing anything novel and enjoyable rekindles romance.

Since Judy began interacting with other women on a regular basis, she reported enjoying life more. She liked having an activity that did not include John or their kids. However, she still had other issues she wanted to resolve, and she committed to tackling them.

CHAPTER FOURTEEN

CHANGE AND HE WILL TOO

"Sometimes no matter what I say or how I ask, John acts as if he is deaf. If he leaves the milk out and I say something, he ignores my comment. If he leaves lights on and I remind him to turn them off, he pretends not to hear. If he gets out of bed last, I ask him to straighten his side of the cover, but he never does. How do I get him to do anything I want? Most days, I feel like I follow him around correcting his mistakes." Judy appeared to have confused priorities. A review of Proverbs about what God expects of women seemed appropriate.

Proverbs' description of a woman of noble character begins with the woman noted first as a wife (Proverbs 31:10-31). She brings her husband good, not harm, all the days of his life, which allows him full confidence in her. She protects her husband's feelings and avoids causing him spiritual, emotional, mental, or physical harm. Obviously, the godly woman broadcasts positive comments about her husband because the town elders respect him. They might question his character if she publically highlighted his flaws, faults, and failures. Nor does she try to control her husband's business affairs by joining him with the elders at the gate. She busies herself with her own tasks.

Each morning, the godly woman rises early to ensure her family begins the day with a filling breakfast and clothes to wear. In addition, she cares for others in need.

Scripture says the godly woman manages money well and invests it, rather than continually shopping and spending. She provides additional family income by selling items she makes. Her responsibilities occupy her time. She lives as keeper of their home, regardless of what work she pursues.

The godly woman knows God's Word and teaches it to others. Mention of her children comes at the end of the Scripture. They call her blessed because of her services. She fears the Lord and receives praise for it.

God holds high expectations for women. While the many tasks God assigns a godly woman appear overwhelming at times, research proves the value. Research documents that people dread idleness and need a reason to be busy because inactivity creates boredom. Busyness generates happiness even when one is forced to stay active (Hsee, Yang, and Wang 2010). God defines a godly woman as one who is hard-working. She serves her husband, children, and others so she feels productive and improves her self-confidence. Being useful ensures her happiness.

Judy's Process for Change

Unfortunately, Judy found it difficult to brag about John like the godly wife in Proverbs. Instead, she became annoyed at some of John's habits and ignored how she possessed some behaviors that irritated him. She needed to stop making John's flaws her frequent focus. Otherwise, she might develop the ugly habit of finding fault with even the smallest of things. Which thoughts occupied her mind remained her choice and had little to do with what John did or failed to do.

The Lord says we find mental and emotional peace by letting the peace of Christ rule in our hearts (Colossians 3:15).

However, we never find peace by dwelling on the flaws of another. We find peace by admitting our own sins, praying for help in overcoming them, and then knowing we live forgiven.

Judy's Outcome

Judy admitted she wanted to relate differently. However, she insisted John would ignore her, no matter how specific, kind, or brief her requests. Asking differently offered no guarantee because John remained free to say no and keep his annoying habits.

Judy needed experience resolving an issue that she considered a genuine problem. She isolated John's most frustrating habit, the one she found irritating before John lost his job. Any recent aggravation would likely improve once he secured employment. Judy described her most annoying problem as John's refusal to pick up his dirty socks. Of her numerous complaints, dirty socks proved a surprise. Socks would appear trivial and, even humorous, if Judy did not find the situation so distressing.

Judy explained that John left his socks strewn on the floor wherever he took them off, and she followed behind retrieving them. Judy asked how she could break his pattern. The answer was easy. First, Judy had the option of picking up John's socks and telling herself, "Picking up John's socks is my gift of service for him today." However, Judy admitted she was unable to view this as being his helper. They had too much negative history around John's dirty socks.

When asked what she previously tried, Judy admitted pleading, complaining, and throwing a tantrum. She even arranged a dinner at a romantic place and explained to John that picking up his socks made her feel like his mother, rather than his wife and equal adult partner. Nothing Judy said proved successful for long. After Judy's scolding, John might place his socks in the dirty clothes hamper for a day or two, but then he returned to his old habit. John, like most of us, resisted change forced on him. It wasn't that he didn't want a good marriage or love Judy. He resisted imposed change. If he was to alter his behavior, John needed to decide how and when to change on his own.

To ensure John realized his need to change, Judy had to stop supporting his habit. I assured her that when she stopped John would change. If Judy wanted to end her feeling like the mother of a sloppy son, she had to quit lecturing him like a mother. When Judy scolded John, he felt like a child and reacted as he felt. Judy needed to cease all talk about his socks. Her experience proved that talking, begging, and nagging were fruitless. The more Judy pushed John to change, the more he resisted. She needed to back away and ignore his socks.

Judy needed to detach and no longer participate in a pattern she found infuriating. John's sock routine required participation of two people for his habit to continue. As long as Judy stayed actively involved, she should not protest if he continued.

Instead, I challenged Judy, "Let John's socks lie where he drops them and never pick them up again. Why should John wait on himself? Clearly, the clutter doesn't bother him, and he has clean socks to wear when he needs them. You are the only one unhappy."

Judy felt uncomfortable with this suggestion. "But what if someone stops by unannounced? They will see socks lying everywhere." Her values obviously conflicted.

I tried to convince Judy that others do not think badly of you when someone else's behavior creates the problem. "So what?" I challenged. "They are his socks, not yours. He is the childish-acting one, not you. Just do not let his behavior tempt you to commit the sin of complaining" (Philippians 2:14).

"But how can I vacuum with dirty socks scattered around the floor?" Judy sounded bewildered as she attempted to rationalize her continued involvement. She held a strong value for what others thought about the tidiness of her home, and needed to decide which she valued most.

"Sweep John's socks into the bedroom, shut the door. Above all, do not pick them up. His socks should remain on the floor until he has no more cleans ones. Once John needs clean socks, he will be motivated to change and do it on his own. He won't need pressure from you."

Judy took a deep breath and shut her eyes. Finally, she agreed to ignore his socks no matter how tall the pile grew.

When John left for a meeting wearing his last clean pair, Judy phoned, seeking additional support. I reminded her to wash everything in the dirty clothes hamper, and let John's dirty socks remain where they lay. Judy needed to let John struggle with his own problem. If he decided a solution to his problem, he would feel better about himself. Certainly better than hearing Judy lecture him.

Late afternoon, John rushed home saying he had a dinner meeting where someone reportedly had a job opening. Although John had a prior job offer, he had yet to sign a contract and did not want to risk missing another opportunity. After showering, John yelled asking where he could find clean socks.

Judy took a deep breath and answered politely, "All your clean ones are in your drawer. I did laundry today. I completely emptied the hamper and put everything back in its place."

Then, John saw his socks scattered around the bedroom floor. Without saying a word, he grabbed a pair, raced to hand-wash them, and tossed the wet socks into the dryer. However, John did not understand how a single item in a dryer requires hours to dry because it clings to the side rather than spinning so air circulates through it. He needed to throw in a dry towel to move them around and help absorb the water. Judy was not to intervene or be involved in any way. Having clean socks was fully John's responsibility. He now owned his problem. He had to decide how to fix his predicament. John wore damp socks to his meeting.

When John returned home, he asked Judy if he would have clean socks to wear the following day. She explained how she completely emptied the dirty clothes hamper and would not collect another load for a day or two. She reminded John of her commitments the next day and was relieved all the laundry was clean. John hand-washed another pair and hung them on the shower door to dry.

The following day, Judy beamed. She felt proud she did not respond in her usual negative way.

Frustration Helps Create Change

I forewarned Judy to expect John to leave his socks on the floor again. John strewed his socks, not because he is mean or trying to force Judy to wait on him, but because he has done things the same way for so long; it has become a habit. Old habits take time to break completely. More often, change is a process, not a one-time event. Only now, Judy knows what to do when John relapses.

After two or three setbacks and Judy's refusal to become involved, John did change – permanently. Since his last episode, John puts his socks routinely into the hamper. Like John, people alter their behaviors when what is done causes them more discomfort than the pleasure they receive by continuing. Pain, frustration, and discomfort work when the person knows how to stop them.

Allowing John to experience frustration over having no dry socks proved essential to motivate his change. Research demonstrates that experiencing stress facilitates learning and memory (Joels et al 2006). Because John's stress level escalated at the time he valued clean socks to wear to his meeting, he remembered how to avoid similar frustration in the future.

The best outcome of their socks situation is that Judy no longer complained. Later, when another woman grumbled about her husband's similar bad habit, Judy bragged about how reliably John puts his dirty socks in the hamper.

Remember God's description of a godly woman includes how she does her husband good all the days of his life. Supporting another's childish behaviors is not doing good for the person when his conduct creates on-going friction in the relationship. Instead, it supports his remaining dependent and selfish.

Some bad habits may even be sinful. Scripture warns that we condemn ourselves when we approve of another's wrongdoing (Romans 14:22), and continued support demonstrates that we approve, no matter how strongly we protest. We teach behaviors by what we allow, what we help, and what we ignore. Too often, we support the very actions we dislike. In such cases, we must first change our own involvement. We must honestly consider how our actions support the other's annoying habits and make the necessary adjustments. Actions do speak louder than words and create better results.

If there is something bothersome your husband does, first pray about your attitude. Then either accept your husband's habit and ignore it without complaining, or do it for him as a gift, or hire another to do it, or stop supporting what he does and without lecturing or pressuring. He changes himself once his habitual behavior no longer receives a reward, like Judy rewarded John by her picking up his socks for him. Money, gifts, time, attention, and performing tasks for others all serve as rewards and encourage them to repeat their disappointing behaviors. However, once they experience serious discomfort because of their behaviors, they choose to act differently.

A woman addressing her husband's irritating habits must do so without complaining because God created woman to serve as man's helper, not his boss or critic. If she ignores his behavior when he forgets, he will eventually get back on track.

Think about His Positive Attributes

Like Judy, you can think positively about your spouse and choose to replace every negative thought with a positive one. Each time a critical thought enters your thinking, ask God to replace it with an appreciative one, something you genuinely like about your husband. Admit all the things you do that surely annoy your husband and how he tolerates them without condemning you. Replace negative thoughts with thoughts of your mate's goodness.

If there is something your husband frequently does that you find so irritating you respond with criticism, you need to determine the role you are playing and curtail your involvement. Take control of yourself first. Change yourself before you think about his need for change. Trying to tell a man how he needs to change, only serves to have him resist and it risks entrapping you in a fight-flight battle.

Let Some Disagreements Slide

Our marriages would be improved if we discussed issues that can be resolved and accept that some concerns will never receive mutual agreement. Knowing that it is normal not to have the same opinion on every topic avoids many skirmishes.

Research by John Gottman, author of *The Marriage Clinic: A Scientifically Based Marital Therapy,* (1999, 96-7) found couples in successful marriages admitted to having issues they never solved, regardless of the number of years married. Arguing determines divorce only if disagreements contain contempt and defensiveness with no attempt to repair hurt. Happily married couples avoid letting a disagreement escalate by interrupting rising tensions with jokes, reassurances, and distractions. Happy couples focus on the positives in their relationships. They tell their spouses frequently what they appreciate. Isn't having a satisfying marriage the goal of most couples?

At last, it was Judy's goal. She accepted that altering her relationship with John required her to change some of her own behaviors. She asked for other suggestions.

CHAPTER FIFTEEN

LOVE'S DIFFERENT MEANINGS

A woman needs to feel loved by her man. What counts with her is how she feels. When a woman believes her man does not love her, her heart experiences a deep pit of emptiness and loneliness. Even in a large crowd an unloved wife feels extremely isolated and lonely because she cannot tolerate such a strong sense of being disconnected or of holding second place. "Even in laughter the heart may ache (Proverb 1:13).

A woman's emotions can serve as her strength but also her weakness. They serve as her strength in how she senses when others hurt, wants to help alleviate their pain, and can listen for hours if they want to talk. They become her failing when she acts overly dramatic and reacts negatively, instead of communicating calmly.

However, if a man must choose between love and respect, he chooses respect. Like her, when his highest personal value becomes extreme, his strength also becomes a weakness. If he thinks his wife disrespects him, he responds by withdrawing. He hides in his cognitive cave, and she can forget trying to communicate with him. He refuses to respond and explain what is bothering him because too often, he isn't sure. He ignores her needs and cares only about being alone. His strength is how quickly he can overcome negative feelings and how he likes serving as a protector of others.

The different emotional needs of a man and woman explain why God says a man **must** love his wife as he loves himself and a wife **must** respect her husband (Ephesians 5:33, emphasis mine). God isn't saying how we should feel about each other. Rather, He directs how to act towards the other. How we must act isn't always pleasant because often it interferes with our own desires.

God created women with a natural ability to show compassion, caring, and sympathy, all behaviors that contribute to others feeling loved. However, being respectful does not come as natural for her, especially when she's upset. During such times, she often speaks catty and unkind. Therefore, God requires that women learn the skill of speaking respectfully, regardless of how she feels.

Likewise, God created men so they naturally act respectful, but God knew He needed to command a man to learn to love. For a man, love doesn't come as easily. To become more like Christ, a man must learn to act in ways that prove to his wife that he loves her. For their wives to feel genuinely loved many men must learn to share intimately, no matter how uncomfortable it seems at first. God requires that we learn what is frequently unnatural and, perhaps, unpleasant to do.

One of them must break the vicious cycle of estrangement and deliver what the other needs. While neither can control how they feel, they can control how they behave, regardless of how negative their feelings.

In counseling, women do not complain that their husbands lack respect for them, and rarely do men complain their wives do not love them. Instead, they complain about what they want and aren't receiving. The Lord commands us to learn what the other most desires because we do not automatically give what each other needs.

Why It's Important

Until a woman learns to demonstrate respect and a man masters loving, it remains easy to ignore and discount the mate's pain and frustration. Being disrespectful doesn't devastate a woman like it does a man, so when she speaks rudely, she thinks he should not be as hurt as he is. When he admits feeling hurt, she thinks he overreacts. Likewise, because a man doesn't crave being treated in the ways that indicate love to a woman, he fails to comprehend why she feels so unhappy and pained with his actions. He, too, thinks she exaggerates or wants something illogical. They judge the other based on their own values, instead of the partner's voids that God expects them to satisfy. The marriage relationship often requires doing what seems unnatural, perhaps even awkward, because the spouse needs it - and the Lord commands it.

Some researchers insist that testosterone heavily influences our natural inclinations. They say that because most women receive low levels of testosterone, females' brains develop a stronger ability for empathizing with others, while men who receive more testosterone have a natural capacity to do things in an orderly way (Baron-Cohen 2003). A woman recognizes others' mood fluctuations and learns how to shift her responses appropriately; a man focuses on determining what he must do to make something function smoothly, including getting back on track when he and his wife argue. A woman rarely shows interest in determining the process of how things flow, and a man frequently misses signs of a woman's mood shifts. They focus attention on what each considers important without realizing what they miss. But obviously, God knows we can learn to love and to show respect or He would not command it.

Being Respectful

Rarely do men and women value receiving emotional closeness in the same ways. Understanding the differences is essential since research documents that feeling respected predicts relationship satisfaction better than feeling liked or loved (Frei and Shaver 2002). That's because everyone values some degree of respect. God commanded men to respect their wives as the weaker sex, indicating that women also value respect.

To act respectfully demands an outward focus of thinking about the other's qualities instead of self. We may not like everything about the person, but we appreciate the positive attributes. Saying we respect another's character or special talent creates trust. We build up the other by acknowledging their positive traits, rather than tearing them down with words about what we dislike.

Respect tends to focus on another's morals, integrity, and special abilities. A husband wants to know his wife respects him as a good spiritual leader, provider, protector, friend, lover, father, and decision maker. When she focuses on her husband's positive qualities, she no longer dwells on what she wants and fails to obtain. Respecting her husband, she thinks about him, not herself.

Loving

Love differs. Love tends to begin with attraction and affection, and develops into some degree of bonding and commitment. Frequently, we respect the reputation of someone we may never meet, but love requires knowing the other so emotional closeness develops.

Unfortunately, our definition of love often contains a selfish, self-centered quality. We focus on how we want to be treated so we feel loved and evaluate our spouses by how they treat us. Thinking about how we feel reduces love to an emotion.

Rarely, do we connect love with serving another because service requires mental-intellectual thoughts.

When we think about loving the Lord with our hearts, minds, and souls, we tend to question what we must do to meet His expectations. We ask, "How can I love Him with all my heart," not "How does God want to be served emotionally, mentally, and spiritually so He feels loved?" It's just a small shift in thinking that makes a huge difference in our actions.

For a husband to love his wife as himself requires that he question how she wants to be served. A wife who loves her husband asks how he wants to be respected and how he wants her to show it.

The Bible provides us with a definition of genuine love. Scripture says that having our words match our behaviors determines true love. John instructs, "Dear Children, let us not love with words or tongue but with actions in truth" (1 John 3:18). Words alone fail, but when our words align perfectly with how we behave, the truth of what we believe and feel becomes obvious. How often do we say we love someone and then betray our words by hurting the person? For example, if the wife says, "I love you," but habitually criticizes her husband, he questions if she is truthful when she says she loves him. If the husband claims, "I love you," but refuses to listen when she needs to tell him about a lengthy event, his words feel empty, not truthful. When couples truthfully love each other, their words harmonize with kind, supportive actions, and the other feels the love such words espouse.

Likewise, when we genuinely love the Lord our words of loving Him are supported with study of His Word so He speaks to us. We pray and talk with Him regularly.

A couple feels closest when the wife's words carry respect, and the husband acts lovingly. When they do, they excuse each other's weaknesses and mistakes. The more positive a couple regularly builds into their marriage, the more negativity it tolerates during stressful times.

What Helps Her Feel Loved

A woman's description of feeling loved differs from her husband's. A woman yearns to know she ranks first in her husband's life, and she wants him to accept her negative feeling, as well as her positive ones. She craves his validation. If a situation occurs where she needs him, she seeks reassurance that he puts her before his job, their kids, or parents.

Love for a woman requires intimacy, and that requires discussing private, personal information, and how she feels about each. She enjoys talking about other people and how they make her feel. Regardless of how negative a situation, a woman can explain how she feels and can do so openly and vulnerably.

Often, a woman desires more feeling talk than a man handles comfortably. Her strength turns into a weakness when she expects her husband to hear every problem again and again. She ignores that God did not create men to enjoy spending hours discussing negative situations. She needs to respect that he fails to grasp her need to repeat such episodes. Instead of insisting that he hear every detail multiple times, she needs to save many concerns for sharing with her mother or girlfriend.

How a wife repeats a problem numerous times mystifies a man. He discusses problems only when he wants a solution. If he fails to find a workable outcome, he eliminates the annoying person from his friendship list and forgets the matter.

However, when a woman repeats discussions about painful situations to her husband, she seeks acknowledgment that her feelings matter to him. She yearns to know he takes her side and cares that she hurts. When she receives a sympathetic comment that proves he supports her reasons for feeling as she does and cares that she hurts, she needs to stop talking. She needs to act satisfied with his sympathy and stop retelling the episode in hopes that he will understand. He may never understand. He doesn't need to understand so long as he's there for her.

How a Man Intends to Show Love

We need to accept the ways our husbands express love and realize that men and women do not convey love the same. Our test is to recognize how our spouse means to be showing love and stop insisting that love always be given in ways we prefer.

A man gives love to his woman in hopes of receiving her respect and demonstrates his love for her by doing tasks he believes supports her. When she expresses appreciation for these jobs, he interprets her as saying she respects him. However, he needs more than a simple thank you if she wants the actions repeated. He wants to hear why his actions matter. "Thanks for taking out the trash. I genuinely appreciate you doing it. It's nice knowing I have one less chore to track." Her description shows him how to make her happy. When she feels happy, he does too because he hears, "I respect you and value what you do for me."

You help your husband feel respected and loved -- not by what you do for him -- but by how you respond to what he does for you. A man does not crave gifts, treats, or surprises – unless it's sexual. Such attention is women's desires. Rather, a husband feels loved by how his wife responds to the ways he helps. When she praises his helpfulness, he feels secure in their relationship and interprets her appreciation as, "I respect your wanting to help and love you for it."

However, if she ignores what he does or criticizes him for the things he fails to do, he tends to stop helping completely. He finds it better to do nothing than to receive criticism while having good intentions.

Wording appreciation for a husband's helpfulness stores extra respect in his heart and helps eliminate any lingering resentment. You say, "Thanks. I appreciate you doing that for me. I respect your helping," and say it often and he will do more to show he loves you. Everything your husband does for you, even when you must ask, represents his gift of service.

He's Not a Girlfriend

We need to accept our mate's limitations. All spouses prove inadequate in their ability to love completely as the mate desires; yet, both act as God created them. Still, the Lord challenges both to continue learning. Remember, God listed loving others as oneself as the second greatest commandment. The command does not imply that we give love in ways we like receiving it. Rather, it requires loving our mates to the full extent that we, too, like being loved.

God created men and woman to crave different types of love, so they bring balance to their marriage. A woman offers connection with oral communication; a man brings physical bonding. He wants appreciation for all he does to help and as an active sexual partner because he feels loved with touch. She feels loved with talk. Love requires her to appreciate his need for touching; he must master connecting in warm emotional ways.

A man doesn't think like a woman. He doesn't talk like a woman, and he doesn't listen like a woman. His blue eardrums cannot process emotions like a woman's pink tongue attempts to relate. When a wife tries to have her husband talk more and in ways she prefers, she is attempting to have him act like another woman, and he feels disrespected. She needs to understand his differences.

In addition, men tend to ignore details they consider trivial. They have no clue that women expect them to discuss things they consider insignificant. For example, you may tell your husband several times how badly you need a haircut. He may grunt, but more often he ignores your message. He dismisses your comment because he sees no way to help. Afterwards, if you do not point out your new style, two weeks pass before he notices the change because he considers haircuts a typical, routine task. Rarely does a man create a theatrical production over having his haircut, so he fails to notice when you attempt to use yours for gaining his attention. However, you can respect that he offers flattering words once you ensure he notices. You can alter this disconnect by asking him to drive you to the salon. By shifting a haircut to a shared activity, he will comment on your new hairdo the minute you return to the car. Remember, he thrives on activities.

When a man discusses how many inches it rained or who made a touchdown in last night's game he relates impersonally. Such comments leave no reason for explaining how he feels about either. Still, he intends it as sharing. He tells his wife because he rates such things as important. Sharing what he considers interesting increases marital closeness for him, and he believes it will for his wife. If she wants a strong relationship, she must accept responsibility for showing respect for her husband's interests as she expects him to show hers.

Without Respect, He Pulls Away

A husband loses attraction for a wife who fails to respond to the things he does for her and their children. When a man lacks respect, he feels devalued and becomes a prime target for straying. It might be with another woman or an over-investment in work, recreation, or some drug. Unfortunately, when a husband invests in something or someone other than his family, a wife tends to complain and criticize.

If she consults a counselor, she learns that nagging is the worst reaction she can have. Disparagement pushes her husband deeper into the outside involvement. When faced with continued criticism, a man creates a long list of excuses to justify his wrong behavior. Instead, the husband needs a renewed cause for doing what's right.

Asking a man to act lovingly when he feels disrespected is like him asking his wife to have sex after he's insulted her in front of his mother. No way will it happen.

Judy's Success

Judy agreed to do three things for improving her marriage. First, she agreed to refrain from telling John the ways he annoyed her. She promised to bite her tongue or walk away so critical words no longer passed through her lips. Second, she vowed to no longer mention issues from the past, unless John could change things. Third, Judy agreed to tell John what she appreciated about him and to thank him for all he did for her and the family. Judy required an entire session to understand John's deep need for respect and to try a positive approach. Eventually, she developed a list of what she respected about John and prepared to tell him.

That evening, Judy waited until John entered the bedroom to change clothes when she said, "You know, John, there are many things I genuinely respect about you. There are numerous things you do that make me proud of being your wife." Quickly, Judy turned and walked to the kitchen.

Half-dressed, John followed, asking what she meant. He wanted to hear more. Judy explained, "John, I respect how you always want to spend time with me and the children, even though many days you work twelve hours to provide us a comfortable lifestyle. I respect that you take us to worship and help keep the children quiet. I really like that you hold my hand when we pray. I enjoy sitting beside you in the evenings watching TV because you watch programs that I also enjoy and not just ballgames, as some men do. You make me feel special when we leave worship or a movie, and you step forward to block others and allow me to crowd in front."

Judy acknowledged how she appreciated that John does not let the children speak rudely to her. If one tried, he always intervened and sternly disciplined the child. Judy admitted how John did his best to get her anything she wanted. He might not be able, but she realized how he wished he could. Judy even said, "I like that you give me all the slightly burned popcorn kernels. Just you recognizing that I like them shows you are aware of little things important to me. I thank you and love you for that."

By the time Judy talked through her list, John beamed. As he raced to the bedroom to finish changing, John yelled for Judy not to start dinner. He offered to cook burgers on the grill, and insisted the kids could do the dishes. When one of the children groaned loudly, John reacted, "And I dare you to complain about helping your mother after all the errands she runs for you." When John felt respected, he immediately wanted to serve Judy by relieving her of a chore she usually did. Finally, Judy recognized John's intention. She knew he intended to show her that he loved her and in a way that a man knows best.

Consider how difficult Judy's life would be without John's positive traits and behaviors. Your life is also better because of your spouse's attributes. You married him because of his good qualities. Therefore, do like Judy. Swallow your negative thoughts and broadcast your positive views about that man in your life. Tell him how you value his helpfulness. Tell him what you respect about him, and tell him often. Tell God what you appreciate about your husband and in your husband's hearing. Tell him in front of his father and other men. Above all, tell him in your children's hearing. When your children hear such words, you tutor your boys in how to meet a woman's needs and show young girls how to appreciate a man.

Even if your husband is not loving you in all the ways you want, it does not mean that he is not loving you the best he can with his current knowledge of a woman's desires. Few husbands know how to nourish and maintain a relationship in ways a wife desires. Inside his thoughts, your husband tells himself that he shows you love in ways that matter the most. Everything he does to help you represents his gift of love. Accept the challenge of showing him how to love you more, and tell him how you value the love his helpful actions intend to be giving. The more you tell him, the more he strives to serve you. Because a man values respect so highly, he needs frequent reassurances that you appreciate all he does.

As Judy would realize, God created women to be their husbands' helpers, and she is to submit, not be his auditor or judge. Judy needed to act appreciative for all John did for her. Likewise, John needed to realize that God also commands a man to submit to her influence (Ephesians 5:21). Initially they found the concept confusing, but this would become clearer during their next session.

I would not see them many more times because John signed a contract to accept a job offer in another state this week. That meant we needed to select carefully what we covered going forward.

CHAPTER SIXTEEN

HONORING OUR ROLE

"But my husband doesn't deserve respect. He does nothing to earn it. In fact, he does the exact opposite." This sad woman exploded with graphic details about her husband. Tears streamed down her cheeks. The longer she talked the more upset she became. "Since marrying, he's gained an additional 100 pounds and waddles when he walks. He looks ten months pregnant. He promises to do things for me and the kids, but he never finishes anything. Recently, I discovered he withdrew our vacation savings and bought himself a boat. How can I respect a man who acts like he does?"

Maybe, you ask a similar question about your husband. If you doubt that your man deserves respect, perhaps you think correctly. At times, your husband does nothing to deserve respect, but then some days, women do not deserve love. Still, God loves you. And He loves your husband.

God loves us with our sinful shortcomings. Jesus models how to love, and His mandate about how we are to treat each other does not include earning respect or deserving love. How our spouses treat us should not determine our behavior. We act as we should because the Lord requires it. We do what's right because it pleases God and helps us feel good about ourselves. Why would we allow another's bad behavior to decide how we act? Good behavior, maybe, but not their wrong ones.

Man the Leader; Woman His Helper

Like the husband who independently used vacation money for purchasing a boat, John and Judy needed to understand submission and leadership. Their negative situations tended to begin with Judy using hurtful words and John reacting defensively. Feeling annoyed, John refused her any influence on his decisions. He protected his stance no matter the discomfort it caused his family. His pride dominated.

Both couples needed a deeper study of Scripture to understand why and how relationships became this way. Until they recognized such behavior, they lacked value for altering their patterns. And, yet, both needed to change.

God created man first (Genesis 2:7) and then woman to support man (Genesis 2:18). God assigned man the leadership role of protecting and providing for woman (and ruler over all animals). Woman became man's able helper. Neither role implied superiority. Their strengths differed and complemented each other. The leadership of Adam and submission of Eve blended into a perfect, interconnected oneness.

Just as God created Eve to be Adam's helper (Genesis 2:18), He wants all women today to serve as helpers for their husbands. Title of helper carries tremendous merit. Recall the numerous ways Jesus helped others, and multiple Scriptures call God, our Holy Father, a helper (Exodus 18:4; Deuteronomy 33:29; Psalm 27:9; 54:4; 118:7; Hebrews 13:6). Therefore, woman's title of helper bestows a blessing on women and rates significantly with the Lord. With God, women and men hold equal value and worth. But they do share different roles with unique responsibilities.

As her husband's helper, a wife helps her man feel respected and valued, and when he feels prized, the family grows in healthy, peaceful ways. Every husband wants to feel exceptional, important, and needed, and when his wife helps him feel this way, he cherishes her and loves their relationship.

Women Either Submit Or Control

Scriptures specifically state a woman's need to submit to her husband - as to the Lord (Ephesians 5:22, 24; Colossians 3:18; 1 Peter 3:1). Peter explains the importance of such behavior by explaining how the behavior of a submissive wife can win an unbelieving husband for the Lord. God knew women needed a heavy dose of this instruction because, often, a woman prefers control.

Since Eve's disobedience, women continue proving how challenging respectful submission really is. More often, a woman tries to control her husband. She likes to say what he does, where he goes, whom he sees, and how much money he spends. Control creates an unquenchable appetite that can never be satisfied and requires the strongest commitment to change. I suggest that, to a man, control appears the opposite of love. He feels smothered.

Began with Adam and Eve

No wonder the serpent tempted Eve rather than Adam. As Josh Coleman (2006) reveals, men tend to stop and think about what they want and how they feel before making a decision. However, most women know instantly. If the serpent had approached Adam first, Adam would have sat in the shade of the fruit tree for hours analyzing the serpent's words and determining what he thought about the suggestions before taking action.

However, once the serpent touched Eve emotionally, she relished the idea of becoming wise like God. Then when

Satan deceived Eve with doubt about the accuracy of Adam's recount of what God said about eating from the tree, she did not need to hear more. She knew immediately what she wanted. She focused on the missing aspects of her life and how much she desired them. Her inward focus on self overpowered all thoughts about God's commands or the impact such a decision might cause Adam. She would do things her way, not be submissive to God. Her desire for control dominated, and she grabbed the leadership role. She was not about to risk asking Adam what he thought she should do. He might discourage her. Eve charged ahead, acted independently, and turned the leadership – submissive roles upside down and inside out. Oneness ended because of Eve's selfish, sinful desire to control and have the things she desired. Yet, she admitted knowing they were not to eat from the tree or even to touch it.

Imagine Eve's self-talk as she excused and justified her rebellious behavior, "The serpent thinks I can be as wise as God. Wow! That would be great. Besides, God didn't tell me not to eat from the tree. Adam claims God told him, but I was not yet created. God did not tell me. Maybe Adam misunderstood. Certainly, God must want me to become like Him and enjoy fruit that looks so tasty. Surely, a loving God wants me to have what makes me happy."

The problem resulted because Eve thought about what she considered her voids. Instead, she should have argued with the serpent that he was wrong, "I am already like the Lord. I am made in God's very image. I was created in His likeness, and no fruit changes that. Sorry, but you are the one who differs, not me." Like Eve, when we focus on what we think is missing in our lives, we ignore our blessings. And, sadly, we tend to forget the heavy price the Lord paid to have a relationship with us.

Likewise, Adam failed. God assigned him the responsibility of caring for the garden. God told him to do before Eve was formed (Genesis 2:15 NIV). Still, he did nothing to curtail

Satan's intrusion. Instead of stepping forward, banishing the serpent from the garden, and protecting Eve, Adam chose flight and sat passively watching as Eve succumbed to Satan's temptation. Adam watched Eve eat the fruit, and when she handed him a piece, he submissively reacted and ate too (Genesis 3:6). However, as Timothy explains, Adam cannot claim he was deceived (1 Timothy 2:14). He heard God's expectation from God's own lips. Rather than questioning what the right thing to do was and then convincing Eve, Adam chose not to challenge her decision. He acted weakly and went along with her leadership because it was easier. Eve spoke, and Adam obeyed and walked away from God's commands.

Afterwards, instead of repenting, Adam and Eve began finger-pointing and blaming each other for their sinful decisions. But God ignored such nonsense (Genesis 3:8-19). God disregarded their excuses and immediately punished them for their wrongdoing.

God requires honesty and responsibility, not blaming others. He held Adam and Eve accountable for their individual choices, and their wrong decisions carried severe punishments. They made decisions that created a reversal of God's ordained pattern for man – woman relationships. Both made bad choices, and God dealt swift consequences. Both rebelled. Both sinned.

And Satan won! Now Satan knows how to hurt God. After such success, Satan knows that to entice women to change how they relate with their men, conflict becomes inevitable. Women insist on things being their way, and their men tag along because it is easier than accepting the spiritual leadership role in their families. Men choose to behave as conflict avoiders. When a woman talks, he walks, rather than standing up for God and insisting they do what's right.

Next, a couple's offspring suffers. If mother and father fail to cooperate, so will their kids. Satan ensures that children challenge family rules, and sibling rivalry creates on-going frustrations.

Woman's Punishment

Eve's punishment centered on her family relationships. Her pain in natural childbirth might be excruciating, but the physical act of childbirth wouldn't prove her worse punishment. Temporary labor pain seemed minor compared to Eve watching her sons, Cain and Able, battle. Eve surely carried to her grave the pain of one son being so angry with his brother that he killed him. Then, Cain's sin cost Eve both sons because God banished Cain for his sinful behavior. Eve's punishment remained a life-long process of loving her children as they tugged on her heart.

No one pulls a mother's heartstrings like her hurting or consistently rebellious child. A mother lives only as happy as her unhappiest, troubled child. Yes, childbirth initiated the most painful of God's punishments for Eve, and for us, because a mother never stops worrying about her children, and it matters not their ages.

This presents two challenges. First, mothers have to learn to stop blaming themselves each time their child does wrong. Second, they need to accept emotional support from others to avoid smothering their husbands.

Man's Punishment

God's punishment for Adam focused on work. A man must fight against the temptation to become a workaholic. Man faces the challenge of balancing time and energy so he advances in a career, satisfies his wife's cravings, and rears God-fearing children. Yet, often career advancement and home demands prove incompatible. He lives with a strong tug from both. Meeting daily demands challenge him to set priorities and master being a stand-up-for-what's-right-type-of-guy no matter how strongly his wife may protest.

God holds us individually responsible for every decision we make, regardless of genetics, life experiences, or parental failings. Adam and Eve had a perfect parent, perfect DNA, and a perfect environment, and they still chose wrongly.

Yes, Satan won. Conflict with each other separated them from God, but God provided another option. His Son's sacrifice regained man's relationship with Him, and Jesus' blood atoned for the evil that believer's exhibit daily. We live without excuse for our sinful choices, but Jesus' death provided a way for receiving forgiveness. When our choice is right, we win, and Satan loses.

Us and Jesus, Not Us and Husbands

Satan deceived Eve (1 Timothy 2:14), and she chose to do the opposite of what God told Adam. She refused to listen and chose to do things her way.

Today, women behave similarly. We fight against another telling us what to do. However, like Eve, our submitting is not just about us and our husbands. Submitting reveals the relationship we have with Jesus. Submission shows how much we trust the Lord's promises. The issue becomes, "Do we trust that our desires will be met if we submit to our husband's decisions? Do we withhold and act independently because we fear something we want will not be satisfied if we relinquish control?" Trust remains the issue.

Peter (1 Peter 3:1-6) provides an interesting example of how Sarah obeyed Abraham's request, and she received praised for her obedience and quiet spirit. Peter ends his discussion of Sarah by emphasizing to us, "You are her (Sarah's) daughters if you do what is right and do not give way to fear."

Why did Peter say, "if . . . we do not to give way to fear?" Fear stops us from doing what's right. Fear paralyzes. However, fear is simply a symptom; lack of trust remains the cause. Our level of fear reveals how much we trust God. As our trust in the Lord increases, the more the controlling influence of this debilitating emotion decreases.

Sarah trusted God, and God protected Sarah's needs. Although Abraham made some bad decisions that placed Sarah in precarious positions, God ensured Sarah received proper care. Years later, Peter praises her for trusting God above her fears of what might happen by doing as Abraham asked.

Submission proves how much we love and trust the Lord. Honoring the Lord includes doing what's right, regardless of how emotionally fearful we feel. Such obedience requires a firm willfulness, and our degree of trust determines our decision.

God Commands Husbands to Submit Too

Likewise, God tells husbands to submit, and the ways they yield show their relationship with the Lord (Ephesians 5:21; Romans 14:14; 1 Peter 2:12, 14, 18). They yield to the Lord, other's helpful influence, and authority. Likewise, God commands a husband to love his wife as Christ loved the church, and Christ gave His all for the church. Such love requires a frequent sacrifice of his desires and surrender of his interests in order to satisfy her needs. When he puts her desires above his own, he demonstrates genuine submission, and it earns him legitimate respect in his wife's eyes.

God commands both women and men to submit. They submit to the Lord and to each other. Submitting to the Lord requires that they do what's right in all situations. Submitting to each other ensures they make agreeable decisions and neither feels dominated.

However, in distressed marriages, research reveals that the wife tends to accept influence from her husband while the husband struggles with allowing his wife to influence him. These husbands fight against influence by their wives and carry self-protection to a detrimental extreme. Yet, when a man responds to his wife's influence, research shows they develop genuine partnerships and good marriages (Gottman, 1999). Mutual submission works. Unfortunately, many times the way a wife attempts to have her husband submit creates a stumbling block for him.

He Needs Acceptance

A wife makes it easier for a husband to accept her influence by how she approaches him. Often, she blurts how upset she is and how badly she feels. Her tone irritates her husband, and he responds defensively. Thinking she accused him of doing wrong, he wants to prove himself right.

Only when a wife begins with words that ensure her husband feels respected and valued does he listen. A wise wife begins her approach using soft words that reinforce acceptance and respect, such as, "I believe you meant well or you would not have done it this way. I respect that about you. So, I know I can ask for your help in understanding . . . " Such wording works better than "Why did you do it like that? You knew I needed you to . . . "

Man's Head but Not Superior

I believe God's assigning the husband to serve as head of his wife (1 Corinthians 11:3) means the husband's responsibility is similar to that of the High Priest in the Old Testament. The High Priest held the role of spiritual leader of the community, and a husband acts as the spiritual head of his family. Just as the High Priest represented the Lord to the community, a husband represents God to his family. He accepts responsibility for ensuring his family remains close to the Lord, rather than letting his wife make wrong decisions, as Adam allowed Eve to do. A husband lives in such a way that family members respect him and want to follow his lifestyle of submitting to God's commandments.

However, serving as head of his wife does not mean the husband retains final say and makes all decisions by himself, because God created his wife to serve as his helper. She cannot be a helper if he ignores her suggestions. Acting as leader cannot mean that the husband decides alone what material possessions they acquire. Serving as head cannot imply the husband chooses what occupation each family member pursues. The Lord blesses each person with talents and all members must determine what they do best and apply those skills. A husband cannot make all money decisions or select which people he befriends, and obligate the wife to follow; he, too, makes some sinful choices. The only thing the Lord cares about is our spiritual wellbeing, our living in such a way that honors His Son's sacrifice, and our treating others well. A couple develops oneness only when the wife serves as her husband's helper and equal partner as they make important decisions, while he retains the spiritual leadership.

Scripture explains there is neither Jew nor Greek, slave nor free, male nor female in Christ Jesus. We live as one (Galatians 4:1). God values men and woman equally. Together we form a chosen people, a royal priesthood (1 Peter 2:9). God considers Christian husbands and wives as prized priests who hold different roles and responsibilities.

Spiritual Leader

The High-Priest type role requires a husband to serve his wife and children by becoming the family's dominant spiritual leader. He leads in teaching his wife and children how to submit by his example of submitting to the Lord's commandments. He teaches how to do what's right by his example of doing what's right for their relationships, no matter his required sacrifice. When a man forfeits his pride, money, and earthly desires to meet the spiritual needs of his family, he sacrifices for the Lord.

The husband studies God's Word so he can teach his family the Lord's commandments. He talks often about the Lord and ensures that God's Word influences each member's daily decisions. As the family spiritual leader, he regularly asks God to forgive his sins, his family's sins, and prays for their needs. Therefore, he must know each member's spiritual needs. He knows if his children behave sinfully and, if necessary, enforces discipline and training to keep them headed the right way.

Our husbands need to accept the spiritual responsibility, and it remains our place to submit to their leadership. Every decision we make as a family that is right by God's standards displays respectful worship of the Lord.

Exceptions

Submission isn't complicated when we agree with our husband's decisions. Perhaps, mutual or shared conformity better describes such agreement. However, genuine submission occurs when we disagree with our spouses, and still decide to surrender our wills to follow our husband's lead. We do what's right and refuse to look back without complaining.

However, submission does not require blind obedience if a husband lives rebelling against the Lord's commands. Read chapter 25 of 1 Samuel. Abigail's husband, Nabal, returned David's goodness with evil treatment, and David prepared to destroy Nabal's entire household. Abigail refused to support her husband's sinful decision. Instead, she intervened and apologized to David without her husband's knowledge. She saved her husband's life and the life of every male in his household. She even told David that her husband acted foolishly.

Like Abigail, if we must choose between being a faithful wife and a faithful follower of the Lord, we have only one choice. We remain loyal to the Lord's commandments and exercise scriptural discernment, regardless of our husband's decisions.

Married, we share our journeys on earth together, but we stand alone before the Lord on Judgment Day (Galatians 6:5).

A woman fails her husband if she remains silent and allows him to do something wrong. Nor is she his helper if she only drops hints suggesting he should rethink his decision or if she nags about what he is doing. God did not call a woman to follow a husband in living a sinful lifestyle. That is not helping as God asks of a wife. Colossians (3:18) says a wife submits "as is fitting in the Lord," and Ephesians (5:22) states "as to the Lord." Sin is never acceptable or fitting to the Lord.

A wife acts as a husband's helper by challenging any of his sinful ideas and actions. She searches the Scriptures for guidance and gently encourages him to live by God's Word. She remembers that she remains accountable to the Lord for her choice of words and behaviors (Galatians 6:1, 5).

She discusses the issue privately and explains that she loves and respects him too much to let him act in ways that God calls sinful. If she cannot resolve the issue, then she seeks counsel from another who is scripturally sound. In all situations, living by the Lord's commands takes priority over submission to a husband's sinful decision.

A believing husband depends on his wife for helpful support and influence because he, too, must learn submission (Ephesians 5:21; Romans 14:14; 1 Peter 2:12, 14, 18). The wife's role requires her to help her husband remain faithful to the Lord and succeed in his spiritual battle. They become perfect complements for the Lord, with leadership and submission based on respect and love. Couples become a mutual, two-person accountability group that encourages each other to live in ways they will secure heaven. A wise man learns that his wife brings balance to their relationship, and he can lead her, even though at times, she challenges him. Afterwards, he recognizes ways he prospered by heeding her counsel.

A wife encourages her husband to accept the spiritual responsibility assigned him by God. Honoring her husband with respect encourages him to serve her, and his service provides spiritual, physical, and emotional benefits for their entire family.

In Song of Songs (1:4) Solomon's bride says, "Take me away with you." She asks Solomon to take charge and draw her after him. She wants to follow his lead. Solomon's bride seeks from her husband the type of leadership God provides His people. Hosea (11:4) describes God as leading with cords of human kindness, love, and bending down to feed His loved ones. Chapter 11 views God as passionately caring for His people and longing for an intimate relationship as He watches for a response. "I have loved you with an everlasting love; I have drawn you with loving-kindness," says the Lord God (Jeremiah 31:3), and Jesus confirms, "As the Father has loved me, so have I loved you" (John 15:9).

When a husband leads as God loves, a wife follows eagerly. What wife refuses a man who focuses more on the family's needs than his own? Like God, such a husband does not demand, insist, or beg that she follow. Rather he loves her so strongly that it draws her naturally to him. They travel through life in mutual harmony. The husband leads in love and she follows, asking him to "take me away with you," because she yearns to live in his presence.

Both Benefit from Service

When someone serves another, research proves that the one serving and the recipient of such service experience an increase in self-esteem and positive mood. They reap identical benefits. Afterward, not only do they feel closer to each other, but both feel more spiritual (Sprecher and Fehr 2006). Because they receive a serotonin surge in their brains, both feel good and feel good about their partners, no matter which role they hold (Heitler 2011).

John and Judy needed to absorb the information about leadership and submission. Judy agreed that she needed to allow John more say in decisions about the children and to support his decisions. She suggested she should tell the children, "I want to discuss this with your dad before giving you an answer." They agreed to discuss differences outside the children's hearing, come to a joint resolution, and ensure the kids know they fully supported what the other says. If the issue created conflict, they promised to go for a walk or drive without the children and return only when they showed a unified front. John agreed to ask Judy for ways he could be of more help to her, rather than doing tasks that he thought helped her.

They agreed to study God's Word and search for examples of people in the Bible living each role. We agreed their next session would focus on creating more oneness in their marriage.

CHAPTER SEVENTEEN

ONENESS IN MARRIAGE

"Why can't John and I agree more? Some of our friends agree on everything. What's wrong with us? I wish we could learn to like the same things. Why are we so different?" It proved a welcomed question to have Judy place their relationship above her individual desires. Still, Judy needed to realize that few married couples agree on everything.

Couples gradually learn to negotiate differences and share responsibilities. Judy thought she and John should enjoy sharing every activity, and something must be wrong if they didn't. However, just because a couple shares an activity does not rule out the possibility that one partner enjoys the activity or a particular friendship more. Plus, a man needs some male companionship time, and she needs time with female friends and occasionally without the spouse along. It's when an activity or relationship creates hurt or distrust that problems arise.

In successful marriages, couples eliminate relationships and activities that make one happy but prove painful for the other, and the husband provides such leadership. When they strive to do what's right for ensuring both spouses feel comfortable, they learn genuine leadership and submission and create a oneness as God desires for them (Genesis 2:24; Matthew 19:5; Mark 10:8; Ephesians 5:31). Mutual agreement requires they no longer function like two independent singles but a unified one, as Jesus expresses in Matthew (19:5, 6). Still, they rarely think alike. Instead, a couple works together until they blend their differences into a unified decision.

Undivided Attention

Working with troubled marriages, I often find two people behaving as if they are still single. They overextend in activities and have little energy left for attending to their mate. John and Judy rarely shared time alone. It's little wonder Judy fantasized about a soul mate who would meet her emotional needs. She and John suffered with loneliness and filled their void with other things and other people. As married partners, such an emptiness can only be satisfied by the spouse if the relationship is to last. Judy and John argued over petty annoyances because they felt a constant vacuum in their hearts. They lived with numbed emotions, bottled up their real feelings, and just tried to survive each day. They never felt connected enough to realize the other's interests and wishes and negotiate concerns. They lacked the personal care that closely connected partners supply each other.

Both admitted they failed each other. For years, they allowed their children, career, family, and recreational demands to come before time alone together. They couldn't remember the last time they shared uninterrupted time together. Since having their first child, caring for each other had become a low priority. Their kids, parents, and career were always demanding first place, and Judy and John succumbed to such pressures without thinking about the impact on their marriage.

I asked that they read and discuss Dr. William Harley's *Policy of Undivided Attention*.

> **Give your spouse your un-
> divided attention a minimum
> of fifteen hours each week, us-
> ing that time to meet the
> emotional needs of affection,
> conversation, recreational
> companionship and sexual ful-
> fillment.**

Judy admitted, "I love the idea of having time alone with John. We never do anything without the kids except for our Monday evening date night; but that's never been enough for me. I would love to do fun things together without the kids. They will gone one day, and I want John and I to know we will still enjoy being with each other without them."

John promised to accept the leadership role of ensuring they made time for each other once they relocated and found a reliable babysitter. He agreed to write the word 'together' on his calendar and if anyone tried to interfere, he would say he and Judy had a previous commitment and refuse the other's request. John admitted never thinking about how every time he said, "Yes," to other's requests, it meant he said, "No," to time alone with Judy. When John volunteered to ensure they reserved time for just the two them, Judy leaned over to me and whispered, "John might make a good soul mate yet."

Without uninterrupted time, couples grow apart. This estrangement tends to begin when they have their first child. A new baby demands constant attention and many couples hesitate to leave a little one with sitters. They forget that it's healthy for a child to learn to obey and interact with others. No matter their excuses, the fact remains, they can't satisfy each other's needs without undivided attention. Unless they make their marriage their top priority, it always drops to the bottom and is replaced by lesser values. Couples say they can't avoid it because of so many demands, but every spouse can learn to say, "Thanks, but I have a previous commitment that I can't cancel." To maintain a healthy marriage, every couple needs to ensure the obligation to the spouse comes before all others, immediately after the one to God.

Time with Others and Apart

In successful marriages, couples find solutions that the husband and wife both support. They refuse to indulge in any activity or relationship that causes grave discomfort or harm for the other. They work at being like-minded, having the same love, and being one in spirit and purpose (Philippians 2:2). They no longer function like separate, single individuals, but as two thinking together to reach decisions (Mark 10:8).

Imagine a relationship with you and your husband agreeing to participate only in activities and relationships that receive each other's approval and only to the degree each finds comfortable. Such a plan may appear that one loses too much, but this happens only if the couple stops working to find a solution both can support. Areas where either party refuses influence by the partner highlights one's selfishness.

God the Father, Jesus the Son, and the Holy Spirit demonstrate perfect agreement and submission and, as a result, they share a perfectly aligned oneness (1 John 5:7). When one does something for the other, their submission comes from such deep love that no sacrifice proves too much (Philippians 2:6-9). That's our model and example to follow.

True submission grows by both spouses working to find solutions that avoid hurting each other. Perfection is impossible because no couple ever completely agrees on every topic. Couples always have areas of disagreement. But they can find a way to avoid causing pain to the partner when they place love above selfishness. And they should because continued hurt destroys trust, and distrust annihilates a marriage.

Forfeiting self-desires to do what's right for the relationship nurtures oneness. This may require you to support your spouse to participate in an activity you do not particularly like but can accept without complaining. Relinquishing control requires recognition that submission improves your marriage. Try rewording the Scripture "Submit to God and be at peace with Him; in this way prosperity will come to you." (Job 22:21), so it is reads, "Submit to your spouse and be at peace with him and prosperity will come to you." When you support your spouse's special interests he returns home happy. The happier he is the better your marriage.

You support such freedom because granting your spouse's strongest desires, that are not sinful, nurtures and enriches your marriage. We behave as if the Lord asks us to take all the love we have for Him and pass it on in loving, respectful ways to our spouses. Jesus wants our spouses to know how much He loves them by the ways we treat them. We allow Jesus' love to flow through us and pass to our mates through acts of mutual submission.

Dr. William Harley in his Policy of Joint Agreement states that oneness is where every couple should have been operating since day one. He insists, "If you ask your partner, "How would you feel if I . . ." and the answer is not, "Fine," you don't do it. His policy further states:

> *"If the answer is not an enthusiastic agreement you must bite the bullet and recreate a lifestyle that takes the feelings of both of you into account. With this one rule, you and your spouse put each other first in your lives, whether you feel like it or not. It's where you should have been all along. You create situations that are good for both of you and they become your standard operating procedures. If you follow it at all costs for a few weeks, you will find it easier and easier. You will come to grips with the temptation of trying gain at your partner's expense."*

Judy and John rarely disagreed on how they spent time apart. Before losing his job, John played golf with friends twice a month on Saturday mornings. Judy spent that time with her mother. They shopped and played with the children. Often, her sister joined them. Afterwards they all met for dinner. However, with them now relocating, Judy could no longer visit her mother, and she didn't want to spend every Saturday without John. John suggested that they replace his Saturday golf time with activities both could support. Since he would no longer have a male golf partner, he suggested it was time he taught their son to play. His son could become the new partner. John suggested Judy join them occasionally while their daughter enrolled in the swimming lessons she'd been begging to take. Judy agreed but said she wanted to use one Saturday to do girl things with their daughter so she felt included. John promised that this would never be placed ahead of his and Judy's time alone. They could do something together without the children in the evening.

The *Policy of Joint Agreement* is not for maintaining control of your spouse. It implies no intent to limit all of your partner's interests because doing so would cause more damage. Both partners desire contact with family and friends. Relationships with family and friends must change once you marry, but the policy is not intended to smother the mate. In fact, the agreement states it is not appropriate if safety or health of one partner is at risk. A spouse should never agree to hide abuse or infidelity because marriage should provide both spouses a healthy environment.

Mutual Yielding Is the Goal

When done correctly, mutual yielding stops fruitless power struggles. Marriages self-destruct when partners live insisting on having their individual ways. Without making a commitment to live by God's design, they live by the world's values. Worldly standards cause couples to pursue power, money, status, control, and selfishness. Rather than serving each other from love, they strive to seize control to achieve their own self-serving goals.

Because of our natural sinful natures, some men use their leadership roles in cruel and insensitive ways, and she responds to his neglect of her desires by attempting to control him. Her reaction upsets him more, and he becomes increasingly more unresponsive to her requests. Both focus on self-protection and show no concern for the other's needs. They live in a vicious cycle of conflict.

Someone needs to admit, "In this situation, I want to be the one to make the decision. Please, let me because this issue is very important to me. I will work to find a way that you can accept it." Even a little humor said with a smile helps to relieve tension.

Judy and John admitted that using the Policy of Joint Agreement in other areas would improve their relationship and agreed to try it. Intellectually, they saw the value. Their next challenge was to understand why making decisions seem crucial for a man and how his wife benefits.

CHAPTER EIGHTEEN

WORDS TO CAPTURE HIS HEART

" I'm a lot better. I really am. Even John says so. I know the way I always tried to explain how upset I am has hurt John and I want to do better. I want to be a better person. Please, help me" Finally, Judy realized that she can change and save her marriage. She can speak so John listens. She can gain his desire to cooperate. And so can you.

If your marriage is in serious trouble, a coma, or even dead, remember that Jesus, the Great Physician, specializes in raising the dead to life. He brings new life to a relationship. Prayer puts us back on the right way because prayer allows the Lord to do what appears impossible to us. Judy's praying for God's to help her treat John as he needed worked, and it will work for you too.

Shape Your Relationship by How You Speak

If you want an immediate improvement in your marriages, pray for help in implementing this one suggestion: Accept your husband 100%, no matter what he says or does, as long as his actions and words are not sinful. Why? Offering complete acceptance demonstrates submission in the most loving way.

When you want to discuss a frustrating situation, begin with, "Perhaps you are right. I am sure you had a good reason for doing it this way, and I respect that about you." Such words stop your man in his tracks. What can he defend? What can upset him? What can he argue? Nothing. He no longer needs self-protection. His negative feelings evaporate. Without bad feelings, there remains no reason for him to counterattack, prove himself right, or flee. If you begin each talk about an uncomfortable issue by confirming you know your man meant well, you remove reasons for an argument.

When you speak with kind, intentional words, God reorders your husband's behavior. His pride and ego no longer need self-protection. Without a reason for defending himself, he listens. Your husband changes how he reacts when your words offer support. I guarantee it.

In your husband's mind, no matter what he does or says, he operates from a good intention. He believes he possesses a good reason for all he does. More likely, if you become upset, your analysis of what you think he intended needs adjusting. He doesn't possess a deliberate intention of hurting you. Judy admitted that she misjudged John's motives frequently.

Credit Him a Positive Motive

Living in the Northeast, John and Judy spent long weekends in New York City three or four times a year. After securing a new job, John suggested that they return one last weekend. As they readied to leave, Judy asked if John remembered to bring spending money. He forgot but said they would use the credit card and told Judy not to worry.

In addition to attending a Broadway play, they each planned something different to do. Judy chose to see Ripley's Believe It Or Not Museum. John wanted to revisit the Empire State Building.

Walking to John's choice, they passed a large sign advertising an art exhibit, and John suggested it might be worth a detour. Inside they discovered a watercolor they wanted to add to their small collection. When John started to pay, Judy suggested that they charge the purchase – twice. She worried about having limited funds, but John ignored her pleas and paid with cash.

Then to their surprise, entrance tickets to the top of the Empire State Building accepted only cash payment. These tickets took the rest of their money. John tried a nearby ATM, but it refused their credit card. They had no money for touring Ripley's which also required cash payment.

Judy became upset. She felt cheated. Rather than appreciating all they shared, she held a pity-party inside her thoughts. But, she did not explain her disappointment to John.

After simmering all weekend, Judy phoned Monday asking for help in explaining her disappointment. I welcomed Judy's request. Her call demonstrated her determination to change.

Judy agreed to use the Self-Revelation Model listed below. The model ensured that she avoided judging John's intent as if she was God and knew John's thoughts. Instead she talked about her own feelings, fears, and actions and admitted she might be wrong in what she thought. The model forced Judy to remove the plank from her own eye before she attempted to work on John, as Jesus commands (Matthew 7:4, 5).

In addition to the Self-Revelation Model's questions, we discussed the use of the word *you* when discussing negative situations. When describing a negative episode, the word *you* sounds accusatory, "*You* caused me to . . ." "*You* did this because . . ." Such application makes the listener defensive. Rather than listening, the person forms an immediate denial. Judy's use of *you* placed blame on John for the thoughts she composed inside her mind, and only Judy controlled that.

Applying *you* proves successful only when offering praise and positive credit.

Judy answered the Self-Revelation Model questions.

A) When _____ happened, I felt_____

(B) I began thinking that _____

(C) Then I wanted to (or did)_____

(D) Because I feared _____

(E) Is my interpretation accurate? Is it what you meant?

Judy agreed to stop judging John's motive, and instead, to share her private thoughts and the fears that the situation created for her. She initiated their talk saying, "Something happened on our trip that left me upset. I want to know if what I told myself is accurate, and I want to believe I am wrong because I know you wanted us to have a fun trip."

Note that Judy admitted her reasoning might be flawed. However, when hurting, many women believe they know exactly why their husbands acted as they did.

(A) Judy continued, "Because we didn't leave home with enough money, I kept asking to pay for purchases with the credit card. I became frustrated because I feared we did not have enough cash to do all we planned. I became upset because I felt ignored, and ultimately, I could not see Ripley's."

(B) "Then, I began telling myself that when we have limited money my priority is the one that's dismissed. I told myself that I cannot share input on how we spend money and that my desires and concerns do not matter."

(C) "Then I felt like pouting, and I did. Inside my thoughts, I called you names like selfish and mean. I sulked and was not much fun afterwards."

(D) "I feared something else was going to happen and what I wanted would again be ignored. Really, I guess what I feared was I would again be unable to influence you. It left me feeling powerless. I feared being treated like my dad frequently treated mother and me. I know from experience you did not mean it that way, but still, I felt hurt."

(E) "Can you understand why I felt hurt? Is what I told myself accurate?"

Poor John. His face grew red as if Judy slapped him. He shifted in his seat and responded slowly, "I never dreamed we couldn't use a credit card in New York City in tourist spots. I never thought that using cash for food and the painting would keep us from seeing Ripley's. I looked forward to seeing their displays too. After discovering they refused credit cards, I assumed we could withdraw money from the local ATM. I am sorry. If I had known things would result this way, I would never have used all the cash. I promise never to go to NYC again without enough money."

John suggested that they plan another trip to New York the following summer and begin the day at Ripley's. "In fact, how about if we make it a long weekend, and you plan everything we do. I trust you to do things fun. I welcome having an entire weekend where you plan it all."

John's way of repairing Judy's hurt was kind and generous. Judy admitted his proposal offered more than she deserved. She felt ashamed that she thought John neglected her desires and did not care about what she wanted.

Judy became upset but not because of what John did. She felt hurt because she assigned John a negative intention and believed she was correct. Because Judy did not allow John one positive reason, she also apologized.

Hurts Can Trigger Childhood Fears

Like Judy, often we think our interpretation is accurate and believe the other meant to hurt us. However, we may be replacing today's episode with negative experiences from our childhoods. Old childhood wounds of feeling ignored, belittled, or dismissed often reignite when something similar happens in adulthood. We feel similar to how we felt as a child when our parents ignored our needs and apply our childhood interpretation to the current experience.

Our mate rarely knows the childhood aches we suffered and unintentionally steps on a painful part of our history. Often, we respond to our spouses as we wish we could have reacted to the parent. Only now, we counter in aggressive attack ways that we did not dare as a child.

Unfortunately, most couples talk about problems and fail to discuss fears causing their pain. They argue about the issue without recognizing the real source of the problem. Judy and John disagreed about how to spend money. Only money was not their problem. Rather, Judy felt powerless to influence John. Previously, she would have reenacted as she did as a child and thrown a tantrum, but this time she thought before responding. Judy controlled her emotions and did not speak her thoughts aloud. She sought assistance to discuss her feelings calmly.

Judy explained that the situation reminded her of her father's neglect. She admitted that John doesn't act like her dad, but still she felt discounted. When Judy shared openly, John cared that she hurt. He had no desire to jump in the car and leave, but instead, he empathized with her childhood scars and promised to involve her in future decisions. Once Judy explained politely, John wanted to help her feel better. Her acknowledgment of past pain drew them closer, while her prior way of attacking left them hurt and disconnected.

Parental Discipline

Perhaps, Judy's father did dismiss Judy's and her mother's desires; however, our interpretations as children rarely prove accurate. Rather, conclusions we draw as children suffer serious flaws. Maybe Judy's mother agreed with her dad out of Judy's hearing, and he enforced rules that both parents desired. Or Judy may be correct. She never discussed the issue with her parents.

Because Judy's dad served as the family disciplinarian, she tended to think less of him. Many teenagers resent the stricter parent. They fail to recognize that the disciplinarian cares about them becoming self-disciplined, self-reliant, moral adults. The parent who withdraws and avoids correcting their children attempts to shun the child's anger. They care more about protecting their own comfort than the child learning to do what's right. No children, regardless of their ages, like hearing, "No," from a parent, and they become upset with the parent who denies their requests. Until grown, many fail to see the love behind a no.

As a child, Judy lacked verbal skills for explaining her desires. When she failed to have her way, she expressed her displeasure by crying and begging between screams. Her tantrums occasionally reaped what she wanted, so each time she faced disappointment she cried and yelled in hopes her parents would again relent. She continued such manipulative, controlling behavior after she and John married by using rude attacking words. Fortunately, Judy committed to stopping such immature behavior.

Assigned Motives Are Inaccurate

Few couples deliberately do things to harm their marriages. However, when a woman feels frustrated, often she assigns her spouse a negative reason to explain her feelings. She convinces herself that her interpretation is accurate. She becomes upset, even angry with him, over the reason she created, and without asking if the motive she assigned him is correct. Once she believes she is accurate her trust in him weakens.

Unless a wife allows her husband to share what motivates his behavior, she lives filled with self-pity and blames him for her discomfort. If she's challenged to admit her error, too often she chooses not to know her husband this intimately by hearing his reasons. For this type woman, a shallow relationship and playing the victim trumps admitting she's mistaken.

Assigned motives create problems because most are negative and inaccurate. We may think we know what motivates another's actions, but we don't. Only God knows what occurs inside another's mind until we ask and allow the other to explain. We believe our wrong interpretations because they come from hurt feelings, and bad feelings are neither reliable nor stable.

Believe in Him

When you think another did something wrong but operated from a good intention, you excuse the person rather than arguing. For example, suppose you leave a cabinet door open accidentally, then your husband bangs his head on it, and responds by snapping at you. You could react by telling him how mean he is to bark at you because he failed to see an open door, and how rude he is to accuse you of doing it on purpose. If you answer him this way, likely, you will experience detachment for hours. Instead you could say, "You rarely speak that way to me, and I respect that about you. I'm sorry about the door." Or you can just say you are sorry and refuse to allow your feeling to control your desire to say more. Many times our reactions bear no relation to the person standing in front of us. However, it remains easier to believe the person intended us harm than to try and understand what motivated the person's behavior.

Respectful Words Provide Reassurance of Good Intent

A man values respect as strongly as a woman cherishes love. He needs to hear respectful words before he opens up and talks freely. By beginning your conversation with reassurance that you respect him, you eliminate his reasons for acting defensively. When no tension remains for creating negative feelings, he explores why you agree. When a man feels respected, he stays engaged for discussing issues. No one disconnects while feeling valued and appreciated.

When you say, "I know you meant well because that's how you are. I respect that about you," negative energy drains from your relationship. Once he knows you trust his decisions, he listens to your requests and your desires without becoming defensive and counter-attacking. What matters is what he hears.

Instead of telling him how you feel, think outwardly by putting your focus on him, rather than yourself. Think about his need to know you respect him. If you place his need first, your negative feelings will dissolve into positive caring as you listen to his explanation. Softening how you begin discussions, multiplies your odds of him helping you feel loved.

A man alters his conduct when he feels accepted as he is. So, tell him. Then, and only then, will he recognize on his own if he erred and needs to change. When a man transforms himself, the change is permanent.

Respectful Words Create Trust

Using kind, encouraging words that support your husband's decisions develop godly submission in both of you. If your husband does something you find annoying or hurtful, refuse to think he meant you harm. Instead, accept that he loves you and reacted without thinking about how his behaviors impact you. Submit to your husband with kind words as if he meant no harm.

Saying, "I know you meant well because that's how you are," requires cognitive - mental thinking and that requires you to bypass your emotions. You know from experience that if you think about how you feel and use words rooted in hurt feelings, you end up arguing. But, kind words that learn his intent change the outcome.

Tell yourself he had a good reason for what he did. Why? Because in his heart, he did. Once you admit he meant something positive or acted thoughtlessly, you can ask to talk about what happened without attacking him. You inquire what he meant without creating conflict. "I know you would not do something to hurt me deliberately because that is how you are, and I respect that about you. I want to know how to make things better, and I wish you would help me." Use words that prove you trust his reason is positive and know he operates from a good motive.

You submit by agreeing he intended no harm. You submit with trust by putting his need for respect ahead of how you feel. When he no longer fears you intend to cut him with rude words, he submits to you by explaining what he intended. Respecting a man encourages him to submit to your need to understand. By speaking respectfully, you develop a trusting relationship, and when your husband believes you trust him to do what's right, he strives to meet your expectations.

Take the Challenge

Do you want proof that standing behind your husband's decisions works? Then, do not speak one critical word for an entire week. Frequently tell your husband that you respect him and trust his decisions. Do not make him take your love for granted. Forget past issues. He cannot change what happened, but with your support, he will improve in the future.

If you feel annoyed, tell him, "I know you mean well because that's how you are, and I respect that. So, would you help me understand what's wrong?" It's giving him the respect that God says you must give him. It lets him listen and explain. Give respect, and you receive explanations.

Imagine how few disagreements you will have once you practice giving each other positive intentions. Repeat crediting your spouse with positive motives and it will become your habitual, automatic response as your brain rewires and learns to bypass emotions.

Assign your husband a positive motive for his behavior every time you feel a twinge of hurt. Trust that he means well. Know he spoke carelessly and meant no harm. If you feel upset, tell yourself that you probably interpreted his words and actions incorrectly, and then, check out the accuracy of your interpretation and believe his answer, and do so without use of the word *you.* Credit him with meaning well, and watch how he strives for closeness with you. He will do it on his own, without you needing to tell him how you feel or insisting, "We need to talk about what just happened."

A woman who genuinely wants to know her husband asks what he meant or intended when she feels uncomfortable. She reassures him that she trusts he meant no harm. She listens and believes his answer!

Seeing what a difference such an approach made in their relationship, Judy posted the Self-Revelation Model on their refrigerator and she and John used it frequently. Judy seemed eager to learn how to stop her negative thoughts the minute they appeared. She agreed that by stopping the growth of such thoughts, they could not develop into actions and their relationship would become even stronger. It would be our next topic.

CHAPTER NINETEEN

VIEW SITUATIONS ANEW

W e all have blind spots. You do. I do. John and Judy do. Blind spots cause us to live completely unaware of what we missed. Because of the frequency they failed to interpret things as the other intended, Judy and John needed a lesson in seeing the good in situations.

When we've been hurt and are left in a negative mood, we miss important information because we stay alert watching for cues of danger so we can protect ourselves. Even words that others say as neutral or positive we assign a negative meaning. Things we ignored while in a positive mood, we dwell on for hours when negative. However, by reframing our analysis of a situation to be more positive, our thinking alters to align with the person's actual intention.

Reframing to Think Positively

Psychologists describe finding alternative ways for viewing situations, ideas, and other's behaviors as the process of reframing. Creating a new view occurs by taking an incident that upset you and replacing your negative thoughts about the episode with a positive interpretation. You exchange your subjective evaluation with an objective one. When you change the way you label a person's intent, you alter your own attitude, and mood. By relabeling your immediate negative interpretation of the offender's purpose, you realize positive reasons why others act as they do. You eliminate friction because rarely do others intentionally cause you hurt. Rather, what you say to yourself causes your pain, "He knew that would hurt me. He did it on purpose."

For example, suppose your husband does something that leaves you feeling uncomfortable. Your first reaction tends to decide why he acted as he did. Inside your thoughts, you may tell yourself he meant no harm or you may tell yourself that he deliberately hurt you. Inside your head, you made that choice.

If you tell yourself he meant no harm, you dismiss what happened. However, if you tell yourself he intentionally wanted to cause you pain, you become upset. You feel distraught, not because of what he did, but because you over-identified with what occurred. You think what he did is all about you; yet, he probably focused on the task at hand and didn't even notice it bothered you. He may have held no thought of you, where you were, or what you were doing.

When you insist he meant you harm, your mind dramatizes the experience by playing tapes of blame inside your thoughts. "He knew that would hurt me." You may tell others about the incident but ignore their comment or even become angry if they offer alternatives because you value your false belief more than truth.

Your false belief makes you fearful that he might hurt you again. Once, afraid, you work to self-protect from a man who loves you. To protect yourself, you must hunt other ways he might hurt you. Everything he does now seems wrong and deliberate. You live detached and blame him for your cold distance. Your false belief serves as an excuse for withholding closeness. His hurting you occurred only in your mind, not in reality, but now you live disconnected.

Such false beliefs cause many divorces, job changes, and family estrangements. However, with each uncomfortable event, you can change her negative interpretations. Change remains a choice.

Self-honesty

Rather than blaming another for how we feel, it is more appropriate to say, "I am making myself upset because of what I am telling myself." We never know another's intention or motive unless we allow the other to explain. Had we assigned the person a positive excuse, we would not be upset, and we could respond with a welcoming attitude. More often, we choose to like or dislike others by the motives we assign to their actions and words. We choose to be happy or miserable by what we say to ourselves inside our thoughts.

What you repeatedly say inside your thoughts determines what you believe. The more you repeat something inside your head, the more you believe the accuracy of your message. Keeping these thoughts positive is important because your thoughts drive your actions. Your actions and words reveal your personality and character, and these determine the quality of your relationships.

Stop Faulty Thinking

Anyone can curtail faulty thinking. For example, in the best marriages, each spouse credits the other's negative behaviors and unkind words to some external event. "He is very cranky. He must have had a difficult day at work." "He sure over-reacted. He must have misunderstood what I hoped to achieve." Only when we assign other's negative words and actions to their personality and character do we return anger for anger. If we feed our minds negative thoughts long enough, we live distressed and believe the problem is permanent. Once we believe our spouse will never change, we choose flight from him. We separate or divorce. However, if we accept that some external factor contributed to the spouse's bad behavior or that we completely misunderstood, we overlook the current behavior.

Maturity requires learning to distinguish between our feelings and our thoughts, and to separate our private interpretations from another's behaviors. Discerning between facts and our self-created ideas ensures we do not try to make our interpretations another person's truth. Just because we think something, does not make it so.

A woman chooses her perceptions of all situations. If trapped in a situation where she finds it impossible to see a positive reason, she can ask the person if her thoughts are accurate. She will discover a different and a positive reason.

Practice Thinking Anew

The first step in reframing a negative situation requires recognizing when you experience an unwanted emotion, like feeling hurt, fearful, annoyed, or disrespected. Next, identify your inner thoughts. What are you saying to yourself that creates this negativity? Such admission demands brutal honesty, but truthfulness lets you recognize how you added a negative interpretation. Your thoughts shift from, "Here's what he did," to "Here's what I am telling myself he meant by it." Recognizing your addition allows you to stop your damaging self-talk. Then, replace that negative thought with a positive reason the person likely meant. Finding a possible positive reason, changes how you feel and how you treat the person. Self-honesty allows you to trust others because you realize that others rarely mean you harm. Rather, your own thoughts cause you hurt.

You build a successful marriage by ensuring that your spouse's negative qualities never control and dominate your thoughts. Remember you, too, possess negative qualities. Instead of acting disappointed, frustrated, or disgusted if he does something annoying, try to identify what could have happened during his day that contributed to his unpleasantness. Then think about a good time that holds a special memory for you, and let this good memory cancel today's annoyance. If you react negatively, you know how the day will end, so think positively.

Judy's and John's Reframing

Remember John's and Judy's argument over how much money Judy spent during her shopping trip? Note how their faulty thinking about the incident limited their happiness. Worse, without thinking differently, negative thinking could become a family practice that their children mimic. Fortunately, Judy and John wanted to think positively and welcomed a practice of reframing to alter the guilt they felt.

Blame- Judy: I shouldn't have spent so much money. The kids could have worn their nicer shoes to school. They still fit. I wasted money we cannot spare, but still, John was mean for talking so rudely to me. He had no right to do that. He does it all the time.

More Accurate- Judy: My thinking of the children's need for tennis shoes that don't pinch their toes is being a good mother. If I had told John, he would have cared. Until John begins receiving a regular paycheck, I will explain my reasons for spending additional money. John was rude but no more than how I yelled at him. I need to apologize.

Blame- John: I shouldn't have yelled at Judy and suggested she should go to work. I am a bad husband and a sorry provider. I blew up without asking questions first, but Judy should explain. She was wrong not to tell me, and it's not the first time she's done things like this.

More Accurate- John: I can control how I speak to Judy. I rarely raise my voice. I learned a long time ago she listens best when I react without yelling. I can and will speak kindly. We are under enough stress. I won't add to it. I will tell Judy how sorry I am for how I behaved and ask her to forgive me.

Blame- Judy: John thinks I do not know how to handle money. He resents that I have no skills for finding a good paying job to help tide us over until he secures another position. I am a failure for quitting school. He hates me. I know he does or he wouldn't talk to me as he did.

More Accurate- Judy: I do manage money quite well. I am a thrifty shopper, and I learned money management from my valued experience of being a wife and mother. Actually, John brags about all the bargains I find. He likes the way I shop.

Blame-John: Judy thinks I can't find another job and so far she is right. Maybe I am a loser. The kids can no longer do fun things they used to enjoy. She doesn't say anything, but I can tell she resents me telling the kids they can't do things.

More Accurate- John: My work didn't cause the company to experience layoffs. I do have a job offer and my acumen to business details makes me valuable to any firm. My family will once again enjoy fun times. The fact that we can still pay our bills is because I am frugal. Judy says it's nice being home with the kids in the evenings. They will soon be grown and gone. She's trying to support me. I can see that. I guess I am more disappointed than she is.

We miss other possible interpretations when our first reaction is to feel hurt or disappointed. We can change our thoughts, so they support our liking others. We do it for all our relationships because being positive liberates how we think, feel, and behave. Reframing allows us to literally reinvent ourselves.

Reframing for a Positive Outlook

Probably the area where a woman thinks more negatively is when she fails to meet some goal she hoped to achieve. No one blames her for not producing the desired results as severely as she blames herself.

When John accepted a job in another state, Judy needed to alter her self-talk about their relocation. Inside her thoughts, she repeated problems that might occur. These thoughts left Judy fearful and unable to provide John the assistance he needed.

Self-talk: The kids will no longer have regular contact with their grandparents. I will miss being near my parents now that they are aging and need more support. I do not think I can do this.

Reframe: By moving away from our extended family, we will have more time to bond as a family unit ourselves before our kids leave home. We will no longer be required to attend every family event and can skip the ones we always dreaded. We can come back for special occasions. The kids can enjoy an extended visit in the summers. If my parents need me, John will insist that I care for them. Maybe they will even consider relocating near us.

Self-talk: The new company may have layoffs. It could be a move for nothing.

Reframe: The company may not downsize, but if they do, John may possess the very skills they need to retain. If they did not need his talent, they would not be hiring him.

Self-talk: Moving is a hassle and we will have to take our last bit of money from savings to help pay the added expenses.

Reframe: Our family has offered to help us move. With so many helping hands, it won't be too much work. With John's salary increase, we will quickly recuperate any losses and begin saving more.

Reframing necessitates having a flexible and adaptable attitude. It requires learning to ask, "What frame am I using that causes me to feel bad or makes me dislike another?" "How could I view the situation a new way that would be positive?" Reframing requires being receptive to creating a new belief about what another person's behavior means and your own as well.

Practical Use

At last, John and Judy prepared to relocate and begin a new life together. With their new relationship skills, they faced fewer conflicts. For them, sharing their private interpretation of the other's motives and the use of reframing proved valuable tools. They committed to reframing their thoughts when they felt a twinge of discomfort. They agreed to look for external reasons for the other's frustrating behaviors, rather than thinking their spouse intentionally meant to cause hurt. Inside their hearts, they knew better. They loved each other. If unable to identify the other's positive intent, they promised to ask what the other meant. They continued using the Self-Revelation Model, and such openness increased their level of trust as they revealed the thoughts and fears that contributed to their bad feelings.

John and Judy relaxed their desires and thanked God for meeting their needs. Prayer and Scripture study became a regular family practice. Judy described feeling closer to John and happier than ever.

Not for Abusive Relationships

However, let me emphasize that reframing another's actions to appear positive is not appropriate when the person abuses or violates you. Never create a positive reason for another being offensive. Abuse is not love. Abuse is evil. No positive reason exists for abusive violations. They require fight and flight because real physical self-protection is necessary for safety. Blindly insisting, "I know things will be okay because he promised never to do it again," allows the person to avoid accountability. Saying, "He only gets this way when I upset him. It's my fault," ensures that evil repeats. Such responses increase the likelihood that the violations escalate.

An abuser should never be trusted without undergoing serious, long-term counseling with a therapist that specializes in working with abusers because many counselors do not receive this specialized training. After the abuser leaves counseling, a long period of testing must be enforced to ensure the person's trustworthiness. The Bible gives an example, the story of Joseph. After his brothers' betrayal, Joseph tested them multiple times before he trusted them (Genesis 37-46).

When violated, reframing cannot be a substitute for rational, logical, self-protective thinking. Instead, a proper flight-fight attitude requires obtaining police protection and a restraining order. The Lord commands that we expose sinful actions, not try to justify or excuse them (Ephesians 5:1). If we defend or ignore wrongs, we violate God's law and contribute to the sin by allowing the person to repeat the behaviors.

Challenge Negative Thoughts

When a situation occurs with your spouse that has you complaining, then you know you need to practice reframing. Until you do, say nothing. Bite your tongue. A sore tongue is better than sinning against the Lord and against your husband with hurtful words. Try to discover why he might behave as he does. Remember he did not marry you with the purpose of doing things to hurt you. Stop negatively judging his motives and see the good he means. Tell him that you know his intent is positive, and you respect that about him. Soft, kind words don't just open his ears; they melt his heart completely.

Practicing with less important concerns works wonders for learning to think the best of others. For example, when the phone rings interrupting your dinner, don't slam the receiver and tell yourself that some salespeople are rude and annoying. Instead, think, "That man is working very long hours trying to make a living." When another cuts in front of you at a stop sign, think, "They could be having an emergency. I hope things work out okay." Provide a reason that leaves you feeling better, not worse. Why allow another's behavior to ruin your day? Practice helped Judy and John improve their attitudes tremendously.

Judy and John Relocate

As they prepared to leave, Judy knew how to reach John, and he stayed connected longer as they resolved concerns. They continued growing as parents and in their relationship with each other. They committed to keeping their marriage more important than any issue where they disagreed. John promised to discuss personal concerns fully, and Judy gave her word that she would use softer words when wanting to discuss how differently she felt about a topic. Their sense of trust seemed stronger than ever, and they communicated better. As tension eased and their connection deepened, conflict over small issues became less important. They let go of what they thought their lives should look like and accepted what life handed them – together.

Their transition proved bumpy, but they made it to the other side. As Judy explained in their last session, "As good as our marriage was before John lost his job, we are much better now. Today I know how to reach John so he stays connected. We know each other in deeper ways, and our commitment is stronger. I love the idea of having time alone with John each week. It will be fun getting to know each other again like when we dated. Our lives continue changing but for the better. I am much happier."

Likewise, John seemed happier. "At first, I worried until I felt sick – but not anymore. I feel secure as if I am back in control of my own life. If this new job doesn't work out, I know now how I will handle it, and Judy will be there helping me. I learned that falling in love is the easy part. It's staying in love that requires on-going work. I'm committed to working on our marriage until the day we die."

As they left counseling, I believed Judy and John would remain together long enough to someday share a fiftieth anniversary. They would rear healthier kids too.

CHAPTER TWENTY

CONFIRM YOUR COMMITMENT

Judy exploded as she entered the door. "I want to strangle her! She controls our marriage. Our money. Our life. I can't take it anymore! Yesterday I caught her examining our checkbook." Judy sought counseling several years ago as a newlywed. After only two months of marriage, she arrived raging about family intrusions. Specifically, she seethed with anger at John's mother. This was my first time to meet her.

Fortunately, Judy and John pursued counseling when newly married. A couple may never learn to trust each other completely if they fail to become a we-against-them, us-against-others, early in their marriage by putting the spouse before all others. They still love others, but all former relationships must now change. Their first year creates the spirit of a couple's relationship, and whether positive or negative, it tends to remain the same for years, if the marriage survives. Many do not.

A new wife is particularly sensitive to her husband putting others and outside involvements ahead of her. If she thinks she holds a lesser position, she feels jealous and betrayed. Thinking her husband cares more about others does such significant damage that many divorce, or find it takes years to repair the harm. As John Gottman's research (1999) documents, an unhappy couple demonstrates their discontentment in the first few months of marriage by using negative labels to describe their mates. During the first year, a couple proves their loyalty to each other or a precedent of distrust begins.

Lord's Instruction for Newlyweds

The Lord emphasizes the significance of the husband putting his wife before all others during their first year. In Deuteronomy (24:5), God instructs, "If a man has recently married, he must not be sent to war or have any other duty laid on him. For one year, he is to be free to stay at home and bring happiness to the wife he married." God stresses how vulnerable a wife is to feeling displaced by other people or outside activities during their first few months. Therefore, He commands a husband to put his wife first because it sets the tone for their remaining years and for ensuring they have remaining years together.

Living by the Lord's instructions, a husband participates in no outside involvement that creates unhappiness for his wife. The husband puts his wife's feelings above others, and by doing so, she feels assured that she holds first place with him. She learns to trust her husband fully. While their first few months together prove the most challenging, it also offers a time of intimacy, new learning, and close bonding.

Keep Love Alive

Couples need to approach marriage expecting problems as a way of life. Even the best marriages prove frustrating in some ways and gratifying in others. Both partners learn they must accept less than perfection because both bring flaws and failings to their union. Imperfections that were ignored or dismissed while dating become obvious when confronted 24-7. Once married, short-comings cannot be ignored, but neither do they require constant attention.

Couples should not only expect conflict, but they should encourage it, provided they discuss differences without anger or rudeness. Being open and discussing concerns prove they want to learn more about what motivates their partner. Conflict is healthy for a relationship provided the discussion shows value and love for the partner. According to researcher, Ted Huston (2009), as long as conflict and frustration are embedded in continual loving affection it does little damage to a relationship. When discussed the right way, differences increase their understanding and value for each other.

Huston's research found that saying, "I love you" frequently and displaying affectionate behavior that supports loving words overshadowed many newlywed problems. This proved especially important for husbands outside the bedroom because the more loving a husband acted, the less his negative traits bothered his wife. Likewise, the wife needed to respond warmly to her husband's sexual advances because a man who loves his wife wants sex more often. According to Huston, a couple's top priority in the first few months of marriage should be to keep romance and affection alive and to refuse to speak unkindly to each other. Negative feelings should not determine how they talk: "A gentle answer turns away wrath, but a harsh word stirs up anger" (Proverb 15:1).

Maintaining a sweet disposition and a desire to share common interests are sufficient to weather the early storms in a marriage. Rather than focusing on a spouse's faults, which ensures marital dissatisfaction, a newly married couple needs to take pleasure in what's going right. Holding strong, sweet thoughts counter bitter issues. Fortunately, a mind that works on holding positive thoughts cannot think about the negative.

Handle In-law Problems Immediately

Sadly today, in-law and financial problems rank among the top issues confronting young couples. Leaving one's parents emotionally and financially can prove a real struggle because often it is parents who refuse to let go. Such parents disregard

God's Word that instructs children to leave father and mother and cleave to the new spouse.

Unfortunately, many parents want to assist their children financially rather than allowing them to struggle and discover the joy of providing for themselves and their own children. John's mother, Denise, proved such a mother. Her financial tactics caused severe disruption to John's and Judy's relationship.

Home from their honeymoon, John and Judy opened their apartment door and unexpectedly found Denise waiting for them. They gave her a key so she could deliver wedding gifts to their apartment. Only that is not why Denise waited. Denise wanted to take Judy shopping and insisted that John should go watch football with his dad.

While shopping, Denise and Judy bought a television and table. Denise insisted that the wife should select all household items and countered Judy's protest with there being no reason for consulting John. Denise failed to recognize her intrusions and how she attempted to have Judy disregard John's desires. Her pattern continued for several weeks, even with smaller purchases like towels and soap.

Denise grabbed control and insisted that Judy and John cave to her ideas. To make matters worse, if they stated not having the money to purchase something Denise recommended, she bought it for them. She appeared often at their door loaded with gifts.

Needless-to-say, Judy and John experienced many heated disagreements about Denise's involvement. Both needed to clarify their concerns and together agree what should be done to curtail Denise's involvements. Judy needed to set limits on what she could tolerate her mother-in-law doing and enforce them. However, it became John's place to tell his mother to stop interfering.

Enforcing limits with parents becomes one of the most difficult challenges newlyweds must address. It remains doubly complicated with money the issue, but such encroachment must be stopped. Any unwelcomed involvement that creates hurt for either partner increases the likelihood that marriages like John's and Judy's will fail.

Having the best things in life given to them undercuts the joy of newlyweds succeeding on their own. Research confirms financial conflict destroys a couple's marital satisfaction and increases their chance of divorce; however, taking steps to protect their financial stability secures their relationship (Dew, 2011). Couples need to bond around money issues, not experience continual handouts.

John agreed they needed to halt his mother's meddling. However, it took several role playing episodes with John before he could tell his mother to quit buying them gifts and, instead, let them learn to save for things they wanted.

Eventually, John set a firm boundary with his mother. "Mom, Judy and I decided that, in the future, she and I will purchase all things for our home – alone. The inside of our home needs to reflect our likes. Judy possesses great decorating taste and should decide how our home looks. Therefore, we plan on returning several items you bought us. We want our home to reflect our own private space. We love you and know you want us to have a happy marriage, one that shows our love for each other. We need to keep our money and spending private, and we need you to no longer buy us gifts except at Christmas. Otherwise, we can't accept them."

"Also, as we told you, we want a child before long. Once we have a baby, we hope you will be our number one babysitter. Since Judy's mother lives over an hour away, we hope you accept the role of primary grandma-sitter. We plan on you being there to help us."

John's saying, "Judy and I" helped to ensure that Denise understood they acted in agreement and reduced the likelihood of Denise privately coercing Judy to allow her continued participation. John and Judy wanted Denise to realize that she gained more by cooperating than by resisting. John solicited her agreement by suggesting she would become their chief baby-sitting grandma.

Although difficult, the married child who has family interfering must be the one to block unwelcomed involvements. Parents accept such a request from their own child better than from the child's spouse, especially when they receive assurance that there is no intent to exclude them completely. The child more likely secures continued relations.

However, if a parent continues undermining the marriage, then all contact must be severed until the parent agrees to honor the couple's boundaries. Meanwhile, a young couple should remember that the parent disrupted the relationship, not them.

God takes a firm stand against family members and friends who behave in ways that damage our marriages. Jeremiah (12:6) stresses not to trust any family member who betrays us, and Lamentations (1:2) calls friends who act disloyal enemies. How sad when relatives damage a new marriage. Hopefully, all outsiders will honor such limits with a first request so a permanent separation remains unnecessary. However, if they ignore such limits, all contact must be severed until they agree.

Create Privacy Boundaries

One of the first commandments in Scripture (Genesis 2:24) is for a couple to leave mother and father and be joined together as one. This commandment requires a couple to limit their emotional, physical, and financial involvements with parents, siblings, friends, grandparents, and even future children. They must exclude all others to unite as a single unit and become an us – against - them.

However, newlyweds do not eliminate other people from their lives; rather, they establish exclusive intimacy topics they share with no one else, like sex, the spouse's flaws, and their children's secrets. They also protect their spouses' sensitive areas, like weight and salary. They respect such concerns by discussing them with no other. Scripture confirms they should never betray each other's confidence (Proverbs 25:9). Likewise, newlyweds need to determine how they want to celebrate holidays and special occasions and set those boundaries before either set of their parents insists they honor that parent's traditions.

To become one with a spouse requires a loss of intimacy with one's birth family and a new way of communicating with all others. The spouse's needs and feelings must be placed before others; otherwise, the spouse feels betrayed. Betrayal reflects the deepest, most painful offense inflicted upon the heart and soul of a mate. Scriptures says it is better not to make a vow than to make one and not fulfill it (Ecclesiastes, 3:5), and that includes the wedding vow. Jesus asks that we be people who keep our words, by letting our yes be a genuine yes and our no mean no, and at our weddings, we promise to put the new mate before all others.

Laugh at Yourself and Family Flaws

Learning to laugh at one's own faults and the flaws of one's family reveals a sign of maturity. At first, Judy reacted defensively when John admitted feeling hurt over having no say about which television she and his mother purchased. Then, John admitted he knew the blame belonged to his mother and acknowledged how controlling his mother behaves. He explained how his mother attempted to dominate everyone in her life and ruined family events by barking orders at other women.

Denise cherished control. Once John recognized the humor in his mother's controlling attempts, he and Judy united around their stance. Then, Judy relaxed and shared peculiar behaviors about her own family. They laughed all evening about idiosyncrasies they brought into their marriage.

Couples who laugh at themselves share a special bond. They quarrel less and accept each other's petty quirks as their type of normal.

Managing Phone Calls

If newlyweds have family members who phone daily and their calls become intrusive, they need to disconnect the phones for an hour or so each evening to share some 'our time' without interruptions. When your family asks why they cannot reach you, be honest. Tell them between x and y is your time to reconnect and hear about each other's day. Just because a telephone rings does not mean you must answer it.

In seminars, I explain that parents can tell if they phone too often by how their child's spouse responds. If your child's spouse says, "Randy's right here," and instantly hands the receiver to Randy rather than chatting with you, then you call too often. This is especially true when your child is male because his wife, as a woman, is usually ready to chat. Her handing the receiver to your son implies you need to phone less. If she does this more than once, the wife views your calls as intrusive.

Honoring Divorced Parents

Parental divorce greatly weakens adult children's relationships with their parents because loyalty to one parent often feels like betrayal to the other. God commands married children to honor their parents, but it becomes trying when divorced parents refuse to act courteously to each other and decline events if the other attends. The child of divorced parents should establish standards for being with these parents, and the new spouse should support that decision. Regardless of how the divorced parents behave, a young couple must not allow the parents to create tension in their relationship.

Honoring one's parents is a commandment, but allowing them to manage your marriage is not. Rather, leaving one's parents details the commandment given by God, and that means super-gluing yourself to your spouse and creating your own separate identity.

Give Your Spouse Options

Judy's parents expected her and John to attend their yearly family reunion. Anyone who missed the event needed a strong excuse, and Judy dreaded going.

The reunion often proved an unpleasant occasion. Yearly, Judy's dad started an argument with his own elderly father-in-law. They made everyone uncomfortable with their loud disagreements. Judy shared how volatile the two men became one year. Both began shouting and their wives pushed them into the pool. Judy feared John might be uncomfortable, so she offered him the choice of not attending and offered to explain his absence. Judy put her husband's comfort before her family's expectation. John could go or not.

If you have a relative who frequently makes your husband uncomfortable, model Judy, and give your husband the option of not attending every event. Why should your husband go and be miserable just so you have a partner? Tell him what he can expect and give him the option of remaining home. If he chooses to go and someone annoys him, intervene to protect him. If things become uncomfortable for either of you, leaving always remains an option.

Advance Preparation

At family gatherings, define a way you can protect each other from insensitive comments. For example, ask your husband to change the subject if your mother starts lecturing about how you needed to complete college. If your dad corners your husband, and questions him about how much money he makes, interrupt them, and suggest an errand for your husband. Agree in advance, how to run interference for each other. Demonstrate that you function as we-against-them by acting as a united front as God commands.

If someone regularly makes annoying comments, decide in advance what you might say to curtail such rudeness. Prepare a generic reply. For example, you might say, "You could be right." This does not imply the person is correct. It just removes the person's arguments. If criticized, say, "I don't always do things as I wish I did." Such words do not admit you erred but serve to stop a critic's rudeness. You stop them by removing a reason for them to argue to prove their point. When they think you might agree, you strip them of comebacks. You control the situation and curtail further hurtful words, all without the other realizing you took charge.

Repetitive Responses

If someone in your life frequently makes inappropriate requests, stop the person by having a response prepared in advance. For example, say, "I appreciate that you thought of me, but I already have a commitment and cannot help." Just expect to be asked again, and when it happens, keep repeating the same reply until the person accepts your refusal. If you give any other answer, the person will challenge your every reason. Remember, your answer is honest. Your commitment is to avoid being dumped on again.

Judy mastered using repetitive responses. Her brother-in-law, Eric, gave her no choice. Eric, Jan's husband, requested favors frequently. He provided Judy with plenty of practice.

Eric, in a teasing way, suggested that Judy should type a lengthy report for him so he could have the weekend free. Eric's childhood friend was in town for the weekend, and they planned a fishing trip. Judy said she appreciated that he thought of her, but she had a previous commitment.

Not to be deterred, Eric's tone shifted. Lowering his voice, he said, "Well Judy, I don't want anyone else to know, but Jan and I had a terrible blow-up last night. I think some time away from each other would help. The real reason I planned this fishing trip is to give Jan some time alone."

Judy repeated her same response, "I appreciate that you thought of me, but I have a pervious commitment and can't." However, she knew by the look on Eric's face that he intended to continue.

Next, Eric landed an emotional blow. "I didn't want to burden you, but my favorite cousin is dying with cancer. His hospital is in the same town where we fish, and I planned to visit him on our way."

Ouch. That's low.

Judy repeated, "I appreciate that you wanted to ask me, but I have a prior commitment." Eric countered with a fight response, angrily demanding to know what plans Judy had that was more important than someone dying with cancer.

At first, Eric's moving attack rattled Judy. Taking a deep breath, she regained her thoughts and repeated her phrase and added, "What I am doing is nothing compared to someone dying with cancer, so I won't bother sharing it. Just know that I can't help this time because I keep my commitments."

Realizing what a manipulator her brother-in-law was, Judy recognized the extent to which Eric would go to have his way. When he asked again, Judy answered sternly, "Don't bother to ask. My answer remains the same. No matter your problem. I have a commitment, and I intend to keep it. So, no, I cannot type your report this time."

Then Eric pulled the ultimate punch. He offered Judy $200 to do his typing. Had Eric begun by offering to pay her, Judy might have accepted his proposal. As a newlywed, she could use the money. Only now she didn't trust Eric. She feared that after typing his report, Eric would retract his offer, "I'll pay you just as soon as I get my bonus," or provide another flimsy excuse.

If Eric's relative had cancer, Judy typing his paper would not improve the cousin's condition or cure the disease. In addition, Eric may cause many of his marital problems by avoiding responsibility and dumping them on others. If so, Judy typing his report could make matters worse by teaching him that if he insists long enough, he reaps what he wants at other's expense.

Many determined people, like Eric, make manipulative demands like, "If you loved me, you would," or "I'd do it for you, and you know it." Such tactics call for a repetitive response like, "I do love you, and I keep my commitments. I know you are proud of that when my commitment is to you." By repeating the same answer, you deprive the manipulator of gaining power over you.

Stopping manipulative control means you no longer act like another's doormat. By refusing to act weakly, you demonstrate value for yourself. Others will dislike that they can no longer use you, but you will gain their respect. Each request tests if you stay true to your values or waver to suspend the person's pressure.

You cannot become all God wants you to be without mastering the discipline of saying no, because such distractions keep you from the work that God designed for you. Jesus instructs that our yes be a genuine yes and our no a true no, and agreeing to do something you know you should not do is dishonest.

Identify Other's Helpful Intentions

When couples say, "I do" to a mate, they are saying, "No," to anyone who would interfere in their marriage. To put another before a spouse betrays the wedding vow and violates one's word. It fuels distrust.

Couples need to work together to set boundaries that protect their relationships. They refuse to let anyone speak rudely to their spouses. When it is their family who encroaches on the marriage, they must be the one in charge of maintaining peace or creating distance if peace proves impossible.

The goal is to keep your spouse first while maintaining peaceful relations with others. Peace more often reigns when you search for the positive ways others contribute to your relationship and applaud them. Praising others for helpful, nonintrusive actions better ensures they repeat kind behaviors.

LOVE FROM THE INTELLECT

D ivorce is painful. Admitting we failed cuts to the very core of our being. The only thing more painful is the death of our child. If our spouse dies, others rush to support us, but if we divorce that spouse, many friends abandon us. They do not know what to say or how to befriend us both. We feel a failure and lose our much needed companionship.

Painful as it is, today's divorce rate remains extremely high. Yet, the current rate does not include those who hide their separation inside the walls of their houses. They live divorced emotionally and no longer support each other sexually. Their behavior shows they no longer like each other. One partner, typically the wife, moves to another bedroom to avoid sleeping with the partner. They may attend public affairs as a couple, predominantly for their children's events. However, behind closed doors, they live detached, and plan individual activities that ensure their paths never connect.

Because of religious reasons, such couples rarely seek a legal divorce. They believe divorce is wrong but fail to acknowledge that in God's sight when they perpetrate separation, they live physically, mentally, emotionally, and spiritually divorced. Their limited interaction centers exclusively on money and their kids. They ignore that God's commandment requires love and respect for our mates, not that we remain under the same roof. Legal paperwork would make little, if any, change in these relationships.

Today, once both spouses admit they want to live permanently apart, most pursue a legal divorce. They file for a fast, uncontested divorce, often spending under $300 and go their separate ways. They crave separateness so strongly that dividing material possession goes fairly and swiftly. They resolve issues quickly because all emotional ties are severed, and the legal decree needs only to finalize financial separation.

However, for other couples making a separation legally binding provides no guarantee that emotional strife ends. Even after the court signs a divorce decree, some couples bicker for years, especially if they have children. They fight over financial care of the children, where the children spend vacations, and how the kids should be disciplined. They use their children as a fight-weapon, their last means for inflicting real pain on the ex.

These couples continue crediting all their problems to the ex-spouse. Their life centers on making the ex pay for how they feel cheated and wronged. Because they care only about, "What I put up with . . .," and "It's all your fault," they fight in court until they suffer financial ruin. The arguing continues as long as either party harbors a thread of resentment and desires to punish the other. These couples could cooperate, but they lack the required character trait. They ignore that their children ultimately lose the most. While permanent retaliation may be enjoyable, revenge on the spouse ultimately proves disastrous for helpless children trapped in the middle.

More about Parent and God, Than Parent - Child

I would be remiss to leave you thinking that every couple who divorces raises damaged kids. In many cases that is accurate;

however, it does not always occur. How a child turns out remains more the child's choices than the parent's. Regardless of how good a job by God's standards some parents do, some of children still turn out badly. Other parents who do a poor job of parenting often have kids who become great adults.

God rewards us for trying to serve Him, not for our children's results. Scriptures promise that neither the father nor the son will be held accountable for the other's sins (2 Kings 14:6; Ezekiel 18:20) However, God does hold each accountable for speaking out if either does wrong. Failure to speak out and caution the wrong doer means both sin. One sins for committing the wrong; the other sins by allowing the sin to continue without warning the sinful one to change (Ezekiel 3:18-22).

Even God's first children and one of Jesus' hand-picked apostles behaved wrongly, because Adam, Eve, and Judas were allowed to decide how they wanted to act. You are not to blame for how your children behave. You caution them and change them when you can. But on your worse, most trying day as a parent, remember that how your children behave is not your fault. God rewards us not by the outcome of our kids but by how we strive to live by His Word.

Divorce Is the Ultimate Flight Defense

Divorce remains the ultimate flight defense. With divorce, a couple avoids the need to change and do what makes the relationship work. While they blame each other, the truth remains that both parties contributed destructive pain to the other's heart. They respond to their own hurt and disappointment by thinking that divorce offers self-protection from more hurt, and they abandon their vows. They could work as a team and make daily connections that the other values, but caring about self ranks above serving the spouse. Focusing on self and running seems easier. They may later regret such a decision, but by then, it's often too late to undo such a crucial decision. "It is a trap for a man to dedicate something rashly and only later consider his vows." (Proverb 20:25).

Loving Is an Intellectual Decision

Love remains a decision we intellectually and mentally make. Love is not a decision we can keep from emotions because our feelings continuously fluctuate. One day we love being with our mates, and the next day wish they would disappear for a while – sometimes a long while. Occasionally, we feel similarly about our children, parents, and friends.

When emotions dominate, we spend time and energy thinking about what we want. We wish others would make us happy, and we try to protect ourselves from pain when they disappoint us. Feelings happen automatically and require little or no conscious thought. However, a commitment to love another requires a conscious, mental determination to behave as we should, rather than according to how we feel. Such a commitment is mandatory to over-ride years of allowing our automatic, habitual emotional reactions to rule.

A Wife Means Everything to Her Husband

The following story explains how deeply men depend on their wives. It describes two men whose dependence on their wives determined their very being.

Two soldiers serving in Iraq encountered a direct hit by a grenade. Both suffered severe facial damage, and little could be repaired. One lost an ear and pieces of hairline scalp. The other lost his nose and was blind in one eye. Both lost teeth. One lost an arm at the shoulder, the other at his elbow. After the men's hospitalization, their wives visited them.

Seeing her husband, the first wife sobbed uncontrollably, "I am sorry. I am so very sorry, but this is more than I can handle. I can't cope with this. I wish I could stay, but I just can't. I can't. I cannot stay." She slipped off her wedding ring, placed it on her husband's chest, and walked away without saying another word. The soldier died two weeks later. The wife's emotions controlled her behavior. She fled from her husband's need for support and her marital vows in favor of her own comfort and self-protection from pain.

The second wife, upon seeing her husband, also began to cry. She immediately leaned down, kissed her husband on the cheek, and assured him, "Together we will get through this. We still have each other. I love you and will be here for you until death do us part. I am thankful you are alive." Within a month, the soldier felt well enough to transfer to the States. He credited his improvement to his wife's loving support.

This wife allowed God's Word to control her commitment, not her negative emotions. She drew such love and support from her mental thoughts rooted in spiritual commitment. By relying on the Lord, she let love flow directly through her and onto her husband in healing ways.

True love remains a mental choice, not an emotional one. And the choice is always ours.

Your Husband Needs You Too

Your husband needs your full support too. Although discussing feelings isn't most men's way of conversing, he nonverbally says, "I love you" by doing helpful tasks, sharing activities, initiating sex, and hugging, kissing, and holding hands. The more you respond, the more he loves you; the more he loves you, the more he leads with these actions.

He may not talk or listen as you want. You may remember how he could talk for hours when you first met, and you may think his silence means he no longer cares. Actually, his silence indicates how comfortable he now feels with you. He no longer needs to participate in lengthy talks to feel secure in your relationship as he did while dating.

You may insist he is not the man you married because he did small attentive acts when you dated, like bringing you flowers. You think he does not care as he did then, but that is not so. A man knows how to hunt and catch, which is what he was doing while dating you, but few men understand how to sustain a relationship once he catches you. Feeling secure in your relationship, a husband tends to become a little lazy, especially during times when he is not receiving an abundance of appreciation. His love for you has grown stronger, and he's more committed. Once married, a man demonstrates how much he loves you by the helpful things he does for the family, not by continuing to pursue you.

Besides, how often did you call him a rude name while dating? Probably never, and you rarely criticized him. Otherwise, he would have stopped chasing you. He married thinking you would remain that sweet, kind-spoken woman forever.

He needs your respect for being helpful and wants to serve you in ways that please you. Learn to depend on him and let him be the protector, provider, and problem solver that God created his brain to do best. Broadcast his accomplishments. Give him appreciative hugs that reinforce your appreciative words and surprise him with sexual advances. He needs them as strongly as you crave long, loving talks.

Keep reminding yourself that intimate talks do little for creating good feelings in a man. God did not put the same type brain in him. He cannot help that he doesn't enjoy them. Remember he has blue film surrounding his thinking boxes. They hinder him from knowing how to express how deeply he values your relationship, but his commitment remains solid.

Share his favorite activities and ask directly for what you want. Begin every uncomfortable discussion by saying how you respect him. Keep telling him that you respect him, and he will respond in ways you value.

Remember, your husband hates being in trouble with you. It makes him feel a failure. He wants to live in your good graces – always. Like you, he frequently suffers with self-doubts. Look behind his public façade and see how deeply he loves you, values being with you, and cherishes your friendship.

Know that his life would be empty and void without you, just as yours would be without him. Without you, his going to work would lose its meaning and importance. He would continue working to pay bills and avoid loneliness, but his lust for success would diminish. Work would become nothing more than a repetitive requirement.

God did not design marriage to be a 50 – 50 relationship. With the Lord, marriage is not about give and take. Love is all about serving. Jesus gave His all, and, as our model, He holds us accountable to contribute fully, wholly, completely. Marriage is about obeying God while we love a man who is not always loveable. Love requires being kind and respectful, regardless of how our husbands act. Tomorrow we may not be so nice ourselves, and our husbands still stand beside us.

By making a daily emotional and physical connection, you reduce the chance of resentment taking hold in your relationship. You increase your emotional attachment by giving genuine praise to each other, offering support for each other's dreams and goals, and validating each other's pain, even if you don't understand it. Reserve exclusive time for each other and share fun activities. Repeat the leisure interests that made you first fall in love. Make physical connections with long hugs, sincere kisses, holding hands, back rubs, and sharing sexually. When you connect on both physical and emotional levels, your brains rage with good hormones, and your relationship bonds securely. You also model for your children how God planned a loving, peaceful marriage to work.

Adjust to the needs God placed in your man and show him how to meet yours. When you do, you receive multiple rewards. You cherish the quality of your marriage, and you can look in the mirror and know you are doing your part to make your marriage a success. Your children learn what a healthy marriage involves, the value of making sacrifices, and the joy of loving and being loved. Such a marital example increases the odds of your children making it home to their Father in heaven. Lastly, you recognize how the Lord continually smiles down with blessings on your family.

Every couple needs a marriage blessed by God, and having one remains our choice. What we do and how we act determine the quality of our relationships.

REFERENCES

Amen, Daniel G. 2009. *The Brain in Love: 12 Lessons to Enhance Your Love Life*. Revised ed. New York, NY: Broadway Books.

Baron-Cohen, Simon. 2003. They Just Can't Help It. *Guardian*. www.guardian.co.uk/education/2003/apr/17/researchhighereducation

----- 2004. *The Essential Difference: Men, Women and the Extreme Male Brain.* New York, NY: Penguin Books.

Barrick, Audrey. 2008. Study: Christian Divorce Rate Identical to National Average. Retrieved: www.christianpost.com

Beilock, Sain. 2010. *Choke: What the Secrets of the Brain reveal about Gettting It Right When You have to*. New York, NY: Free Press.

Breslau, Naomi, Glenn Davis, Edward Peterson, and Lonni Schultz.1997. Psychiatric Sequelae of Posttraumatic Stress Disorder in Women. *Archives of General Psychiatry.* 54 (1) 81-87.

Brizendine, Louann. 2007. *The Female Brain.* (Paperback), New York, NY: Broadway Books.

----- 2010. *The Male Brain.* New York, NY: Broadway Books.

Buss, David, Randy Larsen, Drew Westen, and Jennifer Semmelroth. 1992. Sex Differences in Jealousy: Evolution, Physiology, and Psychology. *Psychological Science.* 3 (4), 251-255.

Cahill, Larry. 2005. His Brain, Her Brain. *Scientific American.* 292, 40-47. Retrieved from www.sciam.com

Canli, Turhan, John Desmond, Zuo Zhao, and John Gabrieli. 2002. Sex Differences in the Neural Basis of Emotional Memories. *Proceedings of the National Academy of Sciences.* 99 (16), 10789-10794.

Coan, James, Hillary Schaefer, and Richard Davidson. 2006. Social Regulation of the Neural Response to Threat. *Psychological Science.* 17 (12), 1032-1039. doi:10.1111/j.1467-9280.2006.01832.x.

Coleman, Josh. 2006. *The Lazy Husband: How to get Men to do* More *Parenting and Housework.* New York, NY: St. Martin's Griffin. [Personal correspondence, 8/27/12.]

Crocker, Elissa. 2005. Emotional Effects of Oklahoma City Bombing Linger. *NurseWeek.* http://www.Nurseweek.com/news/ Feathers/05-03/PostBombing.asp.

Cropley, Mark. 2010. Switching Off After Work: Why It's Important and How to Do It. *Personnel Today.* http://www.Personneltoday.com articles/ 2010/07/05/56112. [Personal correspondence, /11/12.]

Dekel, R., and Z. Solomon. 2006. Secondary Traumatization among Wives of Israeli POWs: The Role of POWs Distress. *Social Psychiatry and Psychiatric Epidemiology.* 41 (1), 27-33. doi:0.1007/s00127-005-0002-6.

Dent, Owen, C. C. Tennant, M. J. Fairley, M. R Sulway, G. Anthony Broe, A. F. Jorm, Helen Creasey, and B. A. Allen. 1998. Prisoner of War Experience: Effect on Wives. *Journal of Nervous and Mental Disease.* 186 (4), 231-237. doi: 10.1097/00005053-199804000-00005.

Dew, Jeffrey. 2011. The Association between Consumer Debt and the Likelihood of Divorce. *Journal of Family and Economic Issues.* 32 (4), 554-565. 1058-0476.

Diamond, Lisa. M. 2004. Emerging Perspectives on Distinctions Between Romantic Love and Sexual Desire. *Current Directions in Psychological Science.* Abstract. 13 (3), 116-119. doi:10.111/j.0963-214.2004.00287.x.

Dush, Claire K., Paul Amato. 2005. Consequences of Relationship Status and Quality for Subjective Well-being. *Journal of Social & Personal Relationships.* 22, 607-627.

Divorce Rate. 2011. The Divorce Rate in America for First Marriage vs. Second or Third Marriages. http://www.divorcerate.org.

Elklit, A., and T. Petersen. 2008. Exposure to Traumatic Events among Adolescents in Four Nations. Abstract. *Torture.* 18 (1), 2-11.

Engdahl, Brian, W. F. Page, and T. W. Miller. 1991. Age, Education, Maltreatment, and Social Support as Predictors of Chronic Depression in Former Prisoners of War. *Social Psychiatry and Psychiatric Epidemiology*. 26 (2), 63-67. doi:10.1007/BF00791528.

Fillit, Howard. 2010. Alzheimer's: Hope on the Horizon. *Psychology Today*. http://www.Psycholoogy.com/blog/alzheimer's-hope-on-the-horizon.

Fisher, Helen. 2000. *The First Sex: The Natural Talents of Women and How They are Changing the World*. New York, NY: Balantine Books. [Personal correspondence, 9/17/12.]

------ 2009. *Why Him? Why Her?: Finding Real Love by Understanding Your Personality Type*. New York, NY: Henry Holt & Co. [Personal correspondence, 9/17/12.]

Frei, Jennifer, and Phillip Shaver. 2002. Respect in Close Relationships: Prototype Definition, Self-report Assessment, and Initial Correlations. *Personal Relationships*. 9, 121-139.

Furumo, Kimberly, and Michael Pearson. 2007. Gender-Based Communication Styles, Trust, and Satisfaction in Virtual Teams. Abstract. *Journal of Information Technology, and Organizations*. 2, 47-60. http://www.InformingScience.org.

Geddes, Linda. 2009. Fathers Aren't Dispensable Just Yet. *New Scientist*. www.oxytocin.org/cuddle-hormone/fathers.html.

Gelstein, Shani, Yaara Yeshurun, Liron Rozenkrantz, Sagit Shjushan, Idan Frumin, Yehudah Roth, and Noam Sobel. 2011. Human Tears Contain a Chemosignal. *Science*. 6. doi:10.1126/science.1198331.

Goodwin, Robin, Michelle Wilson, Stanley Gaines. 2005. Terror Threat Perception and Its Consequences. doi:1:10.1348/000712605X62786.

Gottman. John. 1995. *Why Marriages Succeed and Fail and How You can Make Your's Last*. New York, NY: Fireside Books, Simon & Schuster.

----- 1999. *The Marriage Clinic: A Scientifically Based Marital Therapy*. New York, NY: W. W. Norton.

Goulston, Mark, and Philip Goldberg. 2002. *The 6 Secrets of a Lasting Relationship: How to fall in Love Again – And Stay There.* New York, NY: Perigee Books.

Gray, John. Men are from Mars, Women are from Venus. Speech at Smart Marriages Conference.2007. Denver Co.

Gungor, Mark. 2009. *Laugh Your Way to a Better Marriage.* DVD. Studio: Crown Comedy.

Hales, Dianne. 2000. *Just Like a Woman: How Gender Science is Redefining What Makes Us Female.* New York, NY: Banton Books. [Personal correspondence, 8/29/12.]

Hamann, Stephan, Rebecca Herman, Carla Nolan, and Kim Wallen. 2004. Men and Women Differ in Amygdala Response to Visual Sexual Stimuli. *Nature Neuroscience.* 7, 411-416. doi:1.10.1038/nn/1208.

Harley Jr., William. Policy of Joint Agreement. Marriage Builders. www.marriagebuilders.com/graphic/500_policy.html

Heitler, Susan. 2011. Antidotes to Boredom: Serotonin Fixes Like Shopping, Winning and Newness. *Psychology Today.* http://www.psychologytoday.com.

Hsee, Christopher, Adelle Yang, and Lianguan Wang. 2010. Idleness Aversion and the Need for Justifiable Busyness. *Psychological Science.* 21 (7), 926-930. http://www.sagepub.com

Huston, Ted. 2009. What's Love got to do with It? Why Some Marriages Succeed and Others Fail. *Personal Relationships.* 16, 301-327.

Inslicht, Sabra, Thomas Metzler, Natalia Garcia, Suzanne Pineles, Mohammed Milad, Scott Orr, Charles Marmar, and Thomas Neylan. 2013. Sex Differences in Fear Conditioning in Posttraumatic Stress Disorder. *Journal of Psychiatry Research.* 47 (1), 64-71. doi:10.1016/j.jpsychires.2012.08.027.

Joels, Marian, Pu Zhenwei, Olof Wiegert, Melly Oitzl, and Harm Krugers. 2006. Learning Under Stress: How Does It Work? *Science Direct.* 10 (4), 152-158.

Johnson, Kate. 2012. School Shootings & Lessons Learned. *Medscape.* http://www.medscape.com/viewarticle/776891.

Kastleman, Mark. 2007. *The Drug of the New Millennium: The Science of How Internet Pornography Radically Alters the Human Brain and Body*. Provo UT. Power Think Publishing. http://www.netnanny.com/learn_center/article/165.

Kensinger, Elizabeth. 2007. Negative Emotion Enhances Memory Accuracy. *Current Directions in Psychological Science*. 16 (4), 213-218.

Kross, Ethan, Marc Berman, Walter Mischel, Edward Smith, and Tor Wager. 2011. Social Rejection Shares Somatosensory Representations with Physical Pain. *Proceedings of the National Academy of Sciences*, doi:10.1073/pnas.11022693108.

Love, Lisa. 2007. *Beyond the Secret: Spiritual Power and the Law of Attraction.* Charlottesville, VA: Hampton Roads Publishing.

----. 2011. Brain Research into the Healthy & Unhealthy Impacts of Sex on Women & Men. http://drlisalove.com

Lutchmaya, Svetlana, Simon Baron-Cohen, and Peter Raggatt. 2002. Foetal Testosterone and Eye Contact in 12-Month-Old Human Infants. *Infant Behavior & Development*. 25 (3), 327-335.

Lyons, Margaret. 2001. Living with Post-Traumatic Stress Disorder: The Wives'/Female Partners' Perspective. *Journal of Advanced Nursing* 34 (1), 69-77. doi:10.1046/j.1365-2648.2001.3411732.x

Maner, John, Saul Miller, Norman Schmidt, and Lisa Eckel. 2010. The Endocrinology of Exclusion: Rejection Elicits Motivationally Tuned Changes in Progesterone. Ebookbrowse.com/maner-miller-schmidt-eckel-progesterone-in-press-doc-d370213790.

Mason, Mara, Michael Norton, John Van Horn, Daniel Wegner, Scott Grafton, and C. Neil Macrae. 2007. Wandering Minds: The Default Network and Stimulus-Independent Thought. *Science*. 315 (58), 393-395. doi:10.1126/science 1131295.

Mather, Mara, and Nichole Lighthall. 2012. Risk and Reward Are Processed Differently in Decisions Made Under Stress. Current Directions in *Psychological Science*. 21 (1), 36-41. doi:10.1177?0963721411420452.

Mochon, Daniel, Michael Morton, and Dan Ariely. 2007. Getting Off the Hedonic Treadmill, One Step at A Time: The

Impact of Regular Religious Practice and Exercise on Well-Being. *Journal of Economic Psychology*. 29m 632-642. www.sciencedirect.com.

Moir, Anne, and David Jessel. 1992. *Brain Sex: The Real Difference between Men and Women*. New York, NY: Delta Books.

Monroe, Cassie. 2009. Women's Brains Wired to Worry. Illinois State University *Daily Vidette*. http://www.videtteonlone.com

Nakonezny, Paul, Rebecca Reddick, and Joseph Rodgers. 2004. Did Divorces Decline After The Oklahoma City Bombing? *Journal of Marriage and Family*. 66 (1), 90-100.

National Center for PTSD. 2007. Women, Trauma and PTSD. http://www.ptsd.va.gov.

Neylan, Thomas, Bing Sun, Hans Rempel, Jessica Lenoci, Maryann O'Donovan, and Aoife Pulliam.2010. Suppressed Monocyte Gene Experssion Profile in Man versus Woman with PTSD. *Brain, Behavior, Immunization*. 25(3), 524-531. doi:10.16/j.bb.2010.

North, Carol, Sara Nixon, Sheryll Shariat, Sue Mallonee, J. Curtis McMillen, Edward Spitznagel, and Elizabeth Smith. 1999. Psychiatric Disorders among Survivors of the Oklahoma City Bombing. *Journal of the American Medical Association*. 382 (8), 755-762. www.jama.ama-assn.org.

O'Brien, Ginny. 2008. Understanding Ourselves: Gender Differences in the Brain. *The Columbia Consultancy* (52) www.columbiaconsult.com/pubs/v52fall07.html.

Pine, Karen, and Simonne Gnessen. 2009. Sheconomics: Add Power to Your Purse with the Ultimate Money Makeover. *Headline Publishing Group*. www.upi.com

Renshaw Keith, Elizabeth Allen, Galena Rhoades, Rebecca Blais, Howard Markman, and Scott Stanley. 2001. Distress in Spouses of Service Members with Symptoms of Combat-Related PTSD: Secondary Traumatic Stress or General Psychological Distress? *Journal of Family Psychology*. 25 (4), 461-469. doi:10.1037/a0023994.

Robert Wood Johnson Foundation. 2007. University Mental Health Clinicians Treat Oklahoma City Bombing Victims, Become

Experts on Treating Terror Victims.
http://www.rwif.org/reports/grr/028142.htm

Schoenfeld, Elizabeth, Carrie Bredow, and Ted Huston. 2013. Growing Old Together: Compassionate Love and Health in Older Adulthood. *Journal of Social and Personal Relationships*. September24, 2013 0: 0265407513503596v1-265407513503596

Schulz, Marc, Philip Cowan, Carolyn Pape, and Richard Brennan. 2004. Coming Home Upset: Gender, Marital Satisfaction, and the Daily Spillover of Workday Experience Into Couple Interactions. Abstract. *Journal of Family Psychology*.18 (1), 250-63.

Slatcher, Richard, Theodore Robles, Rena Repetti, and Michelle Fellows. 2010. Momentary Work Worries, Marital Disclosure, and Salivary Cortisol Among Parents of Young Children. Abstract. *Psychosomatic Medicine*.72 (9), 887-896. http://www.ncbi.nlm.nih.gov/pubmed/20841560.

Solomon, Zahava, Y. Neria, A, Ohry, M. Waysman, and K. Ginzburg, K. 1994. PTSD among Israeli Former Prisoners of War and Soldiers with Combat Stress Reaction: A Longitudinal Study. Abstract. *American Journal of Psychiatry*. 151(4), 554-559.

Solomon, Zahava., R. Dekel, and G. Zerach, G., 2008. The Relationship between Posttraumatic Stress Symptom Clusters and Marital Intimacy among War Veterans. *Journal of Family Psychology*. 22 (5) 659-666. doi:10.1037/a0013596.

Sprecher, Susan, and Beverly Fehr. 2006. Enhancement of Mood and Self-Esteem As a Result of Giving and Receiving Compassionate Love. *Current Research in Social Psychology*.11 (16), 227-243.

Stosney, Steven. Love Without Hurt Boot Camp: Anger and Violence Regulations. Presented at annual meeting Smart Marriages Conference. 2007. Denver CO.

Tannen, Deborah. 1991. *You Just don't Understand: Women and Men in Conversation*. New York, NY: Ballantine Books.

Vilaythong, Alexander, Randolph Arnau, David Rosen, and Nathan *International Journal of Humor Research*. 16 (1), 79-89.

Walderhaug, Espen, Andres Magnusson, Alexander Neumeister, Jaakko Lappalainen, Hilde Lunde, Helge Refsum, and

Nils Landro. 2007. Interactive Effects of Sex and 5-HTTLPR on Mood and Impulsivity During Tryptophan Depletion in Healthy People. *Biological Psychiatry.* 62 (6).
http://www.elsevier.com/wps/find/authored_newsitem.

Wang, Jiongjiong, Marc Korczykowski, Hengyi Rao,Yong Fan, John Pluta, Ruben Gur, Bruce McEwen, and John Detre. 2007. Gender Difference in Neural Response to Psychological Stress. Abstract. *Social Cognitive Neuroscience.* 2 (3), 227-239.

INDEX

ABOUT DR. KIRK

Dr. Wyveta Kirk is a licensed psychologist. Her specialty is helping people live fuller lives and couples develop a closer connection. She's spent hours counseling, teaching, coaching, consulting, and conducting seminars. She writes for a series of magazines.

Dr. Kirk can develop a program for you that fits your needs or use one of her tailor-made seminars:
Women Talk Men Walk
Help Your Child Feel Loved and Remain Faithful to the Lord
Manage Anger
Motivate Others and Yourself

To inquire about her availability for conducting a program contact her at www.wyvetakirk.com

Other books by Dr. Kirk:
Life Cycle and Career Stages of High Achieving Women
Up: It's the Only Way to Go
Little Rock Secret

Made in the USA
San Bernardino, CA
18 May 2014